TONI MORRISON'S
Developing
Class Consciousness

TONI MORRISON'S
Developing
Class Consciousness

Doreatha Drummond Mbalia

Selinsgrove: Susquehanna University Press
London and Toronto: Associated University Presses

Associated University Presses
440 Forsgate Drive
Cranbury, NJ 08512

Associated University Presses
25 Sicilian Avenue
London WC1A 2QH, England

Associated University Presses
P.O. Box 39, Clarkson Pstl. Stn.
Mississauga, Ontario,
L5J 3X9 Canada

The paper used in this publication meets the requirements of the American National Standard for Permanence of Paper for Printed Library Materials Z39.48-1984.

Library of Congress Cataloging-in-Publication Data

Mbalia, Doreatha D.
    Toni Morrison's developing class consciousness / Doreatha Drummond Mbalia.
        p.   cm.
    Includes bibliographical references and index.
    ISBN 0-945636-17-2 (alk. paper)
    1. Morrison, Toni—Criticism and interpretation.   2. Morrison, Toni—Political and social views.   3. Social classes in literature.
I. Title.
PS3563.08749Z77   1991
813'.54—dc20   90-50402
                                                                                  CIP

SECOND PRINTING 1994

PRINTED IN THE UNITED STATES OF AMERICA

To all people of African descent,
with love and commitment

Contents

Preface

I first became aware of developmental patterns in Toni Morrison's canon after teaching her novels for a number of years. It has always been my practice to reread literary works along with the students in my classes no matter how often I might have already read them. This practice of rereading, as well as my habit of letting the classroom force me to analyze elements of works that I am otherwise too lazy to analyze, helped me to spot these patterns.

In each of her novels, Morrison explores some aspect of and/or solution to the oppression afflicting African people. *The Bluest Eye* examines racism; *Sula*, gender oppression; *Song of Solomon*, the necessity of knowing one's family, community, and heritage; *Tar Baby*, the class contradictions that keep African people divided; and *Beloved*, the solution that will help solve the class exploitation and racial oppression of African people.

While commendable, the exploration of these various themes did not seem extraordinary until I saw the thread that runs through and connects novel after novel. One work picks up where the other one leaves off, thematically and structurally.

Certainly, no one could choose and develop such themes as racism, gender oppression, the importance of knowing one's history in determining one's identity, class exploitation of and class contradictions within the African race, and collective struggle without herself having a commitment to struggle for African people. And certainly no one would be concerned enough to shape her works into narrative structures that enhance the themes without herself being interested in turning theory into practice. If the works didn't tell me this, the many interviews and various critical essays on Morrison—once pieced together—did.

Assured of Toni Morrison's increasing commitment to help solve the problems of African people, I began to think about the particular nature of the evolutionary pattern—why, for example,

Morrison examines problems of race and gender oppression before exploring class contradictions within the race. It became clear that Morrison was gaining knowledge as she experienced life, read about it, wrote about it, and thought about what she wrote. With each succeeding novel, she herself was developing, and her works chronicle this development!

Next, I wanted to know what other elements—other than the reading and writing processes—were involved in Toni Morrison's increasing commitment to struggle for African people. Family background, historical and current events, personal and professional experiences, and literary predecessors seem to have contributed to her development.

Accepting Morrison's comment—if there were better critics, there would be better writers—as an invitation, I thought it necessary to devote the final part of the study to exploring elements of Morrison's canon that are left undeveloped. The exploration is undertaken only in an attempt, like Morrison's, to struggle for a solution to the plight of African people.

Acknowledgments

I would like to thank the following individuals and the organization that made this work possible:

Richard K. Barksdale, for offering guidance throughout.
The Institute on Race and Ethnicity at the University of Wisconsin, for providing the necessary financial support and time.
Clenora Hudson, for making available to me some of the important critical works on Toni Morrison.
The Mbalia Family, for excusing my many physical, sometimes mental, absences.
The struggle of African people, for giving me the ideological perspective needed to write such a study.

TONI MORRISON'S
Developing
Class Consciousness

1
Nkrumaism and the Novels of Toni Morrison

Fundamentally, there are two distinct and opposing world views: the materialist and the idealist. The materialist world view holds that matter, reality that is not conscious, is primary and existed before mind, reality that is conscious. The idealist world view holds that mind is primary and existed before matter. One's epistemological choice between these two viewpoints has everything to do with how he or she perceives events and conducts his or her life. For example, an idealist, believing that the world was created and is guided by a supreme being, may feel unequipped to change conditions in society while the materialist, understanding that a change in the material conditions of society will bring about a change in one's thinking, may feel obligated to struggle for change. This study is based on a materialist world view.

From a materialist perspective, literature is a product of the society in which it is produced, arising from and dependent on the material conditions of the society. Documenting the dialectical relationship between the material forces in society and the ideas that pervade that society, European economist Emile Burns writes: "When the form of production changed—for example from feudalism to capitalism—the institution and ideas also changed."[1] And when the institutions and ideas change so does the literature. According to African critic and novelist Thiong'O Wa Ngugi, literature is "given impetus, shape, direction and even area of concern by social, political and economic forces in a particular society."[2] Of course, dialectically, literature can in turn help shape the particular society in which one lives. Again, Burns writes: "Although ideas can only arise from material conditions, when they do arise they certainly exert an influence on [people's] actions and therefore on the course of things."[3]

Since literature is mainly born out of those ideas prevalent in society, it can either reflect a ruling-class perspective or a people-class perspective. When that literature reflects a ruling class perspective under a capitalist economic system, it primarily focuses on the profit and well-being of only a small sector of the population. When that literature reflects a people-class perspective, it primarily focuses on the welfare of the exploited and oppressed majority. Toni Morrison's novels are people-class oriented. All of them are concerned with the exploited and oppressed condition of African people.

Just as the literary writer's ideas arise from material conditions in society, so the critic's methodology or tools of analysis arise from those same conditions. This methodology can reflect either a ruling-class or a people-class perspective. If it is derived out of a concern for the exploited masses, it will have a people-class orientation. It will be an analysis based on the general laws that govern both the natural and human-made environments, as well as an analysis based on the particular history of the people about whom the literature is written, in this case African people. Only then can it uncover the truisms and dispel the myths that serve to keep African people oppressed and exploited. Then, too, if used to analyze a body of work like Morrison's, which is essentially people-oriented in nature, the methodology serves as a vehicle in which to bring together author and critic in service to the interests of African people.

The method of analysis used in this study is people-oriented in general and Nkrumaist in particular. Nkrumaism is an ideology that applies the universal laws of nature to the particular conditions of Africa and African people scattered throughout the world. Specifically, it uses dialectical and historical materialism first to explain the uniqueness of the African's oppression, an oppression grounded in race and class, and second to propose a viable solution to that oppression.

Dialectical materialism asserts that matter is primary and that all things are knowable. It consists of four basic principles: (1) everything and everyone are interdependent; (2) everything and everyone change (develop); (3) these changes gradually accumulate to a point, and then a qualitatively new reality appears; and

(4) such changes occur because there are internal conflicts or contradictions in nature (including human nature) and society. Historical materialism is an awareness and approach to "society not only as it exists here and now, but as it has existed in the past and as it is developing as the result of its internal contradictions."[4] In other words, it is the application of the principles of dialectical materialism to the study of society and its history.

Toni Morrison's novels reflect her awareness of materialist concepts. In regard to dialectical materialism, her novels are evolutionary; they are interconnected; they reflect quantitative changes, some even qualitative leaps in the author's consciousness; and they reflect contradictions within and between them. Her canon also documents her increasing understanding of the role of historical materialism in discovering the source of and the solution to the African's oppression. For with each succeeding novel she demonstrates her increasing clarity of the need for Africans to know their history, their historical place in society as it has developed and as it is now, before they can forge a better future. Next, her literature reveals her understanding that while the African suffers equally from class exploitation and race oppression, the latter is born out of the former. Finally, it illustrates her understanding that the gender oppression of African women is the result of the African male's class exploitation and race oppression. Thus, as _Tar Baby_ and _Beloved_ clearly indicate, it is the economic system of capitalism, characterized by the exploitation of one group of people by another, that gives birth to and continues to fuel racism and sexism. It is neither racism nor sexism but capitalism that is the primary enemy of African people.

As an appropriate prerequisite for appreciating Morrison's developing class consciousness, one must first understand the nature of capitalism as Morrison herself began to understand it.

Capitalism is an economic system characterized by "the concentration in a few hands of the ownership of the means of producing wealth and by unequal distribution of the products of human labour."[5] Thus, it is a system

> which divides society into classes [sections of people who get their living in the same way], one which carries out the actual process of production (slave, serf, wage-worker), while the other (slave-owner,

lord, capitalist employer) enjoys a part of the product without having to work to produce it.[6]

The class that owns and/or controls the means of production (e.g., the industries, mines, corporations) is called the ruling or capitalist class. To rule society simply means organizing it to serve the interests of only one class of people and imposing the will of this group on all other groups, whether they agree or not.[7] Ultimately, the objective of the ruling class is to convince others that its rule is the most just. If the objective is accomplished, the ruling class secures its place in the society and thus continues its exploitation with few opposing disturbances.

In any society in which the interests of only a small sector of the population are considered, gross injustices are present. Under capitalism, for example, there exists a permanent sector of unemployed people, periodic economic crisis, "incredible poverty in the midst of wealth and wastage," deviant behavior based on placing individual interests above group interests (social responsibility), and racism.[8]

It is Morrison's growing awareness of these inherent characteristics of capitalism that helps her to understand that racism is an integral part of the capitalist mode of production and, therefore, to get rid of the latter is to do away with the former. There is ample evidence to prove that racism is a by-product of capitalism.

First, Walter Rodney defuses the myth that racism was the initial cause of the enslavement of African people and, by doing so, effectively negates the argument of those nationalists who say that racism is the primary cause of their oppression today. According to Rodney, Africans were enslaved "for economic reasons, so that their labour power could be exploited."[9] Then resulted racism, the doctrine based on "the assumption that psychological traits and capacities are determined by biological race . . . and a belief in the inherent superiority of a particular race and its right to dominion over others."[10] In his words,

[After] having been utterly dependent on African labour, Europeans at home and abroad found it necessary to rationalise that exploitation in racist terms as well. Oppression follows logically from exploitation, so as to guarantee the latter.[11]

The economic system of slavery, an early form of capitalism, was the cause of racism rather than the result of it. Dr. Kwame Nkrumah confirms Rodney's analysis when he writes: "It was only with capitalist economic penetration that the master-servant relationship emerged, and with it, racism, colour prejudice and apartheid."[12] Finally, the economist Eric Williams offers indisputable facts to illustrate that racism was the result of the exploitation of the African's labor. He points out that the enslavement of the African had everything to do with "the cheapness of labor," not the color of the laborer's skin:

> Racial differences made it easier to justify and rationalize Negro slavery. . . . Finally, and this was the decisive factor, the Negro slave was cheaper. The money which procured a white man's service for ten years could buy a Negro for life.[13]

Williams substantiates this premise by examining the rise of capitalism. Offering convincing facts, he proves that the early European capitalists were willing to exploit the labor power of any group of people—even their own—to make a handsome profit. Two such groups of exploited laborers were the white indentured servants and the native American Indians. Neither made efficient laborers. White indentured servants, for instance, could escape and easily blend in with the rest of the population. Moreover, their supply was quite limited. On the other hand, the Indian population

> rapidly succumbed to the excessive labor demanded of them, the insufficient diet, the white man's diseases, and their inability to adjust themselves to the new way of life. . . . Their constitution and temperament were ill-adapted to the rigors of plantation slavery.[14]

All of these factors, according to Williams, confirm that racism stems from class exploitation.

However, to state that racism was the consequence of the European's quest for greater profits is not to imply that racism did not ultimately become a concomitant reason for oppressing African people. Morrison, in *Song of Solomon*, seems aware of this fact. According to Rodney, "Oppression of African people on purely racial grounds accompanied, strengthened and became indistinguishable from oppression for economic reasons."[15] Nkrumah, too, believed that the African suffered from a nation-class oppression. In analyzing the African's plight in the United States, he wrote: "Race is inextricably linked with class exploitation; in a racist-capitalist power structure, capitalist exploitation and race oppression are complementary, the removal of one ensures the removal of the other."[16] Rodney and Nkrumah agree, however, that while the African suffers equally from both, racism cannot exist under a nonexploitive economic system. Therefore, capitalism—in all its forms—must be the African's primary target of attack.

By the time she writes *Tar Baby*, Toni Morrison has become increasingly aware of capitalism as the African's primary enemy, largely through reading the works of class-conscious Africans, experiencing and contemplating the minimal results of the struggle against racism without regard for the system that produced it, and perceiving the negligible changes in the lives of the masses of African people. At first, like most Africans, she saw racism as the cause of the African's dilemma in the United States. Her first novel, *The Bluest Eye* (1970), serves as proof of her low level of class consciousness at the beginning of her writing career. Interestingly enough, it was written during the time when African people in the United States were waging a national struggle against racism. However, like most conscious Africans who lived through and participated in the Civil Rights Struggle, she is unsatisfied with the notion that to remove signs of segregation ensures the destruction of racism. Thus, in *Sula* (1973), her second novel, Morrison—again like many Africans in the United States—turns her attention to securing individual rights in general and women's rights in particular. This switch in thematic emphasis suggests that she sees the lack of individual rights as the primary cause of the African's oppression. But as the ending of *Sula* suggests, Morrison rejects this assumption as well.

Song of Solomon (1977) marks a qualitative leap in Morrison's consciousness. Written just after the publication of Alex Haley's *Roots*, it illustrates the importance of Africans' awareness and acceptance of their history, for without knowing where they have been, Africans do not know where they are going.[17] *Song of*

Solomon is important for another reason. Morrison tells us that knowledge is not enough. Africans conscious of their history must assume the responsibility of politically educating their people. In the author's words, "You can never fly away and leave a body."[18] Written after she had edited Chinweizu's The West and the Rest of Us, a work that condemns those petty bourgeois Africans who settle for individual handouts from their oppressors while the rest of their people wallow in poverty, Song of Solomon emphasizes that knowledge, acceptance, and commitment are needed to help liberate an oppressed people.

In Tar Baby (1981), Morrison reveals her understanding of the role capitalism plays in the African's oppression and examines one alternative—a return to a traditional African lifestyle. Unfortunately, such a solution, as the novel documents, is just as impossible as it is undesirable. For the idea of returning to a precolonial, preslavery existence is tantamount to asking the African to erase the experiences and consciousness of five hundred years, in essence to metamorphose into one of the blind horsemen of the Isle des Chevaliers.

African people can only extract the positive from their past, such as unity in struggle, in order to build the future. This is the message conveyed in her most conscious work to date, Beloved (1987). The negative, appropriately symbolized by a ghost, must be rejected.

As her canon demonstrates, Morrison, in learning of, experiencing, writing about, and contemplating the crisis of African people, reexamines, refines, and rejects early assumptions about the identity of the primary enemy of African people. Moreover, her continual thematic reexamination causes her to reevaluate her structure as well. Thus, Morrison's works reflect a thematic and a structural evolution that coincide with her own growing class consciousness. As her knowledge of the dialectical way in which the laws of nature apply to society increases, she will move from a weak to a strong class analysis, always recognizing the role of race and sex in the African's oppression. Too, she will restructure her texts to reflect the societal structure that is best able to meet the needs of the African masses.

It is an interesting comment on Morrison's own increasing class consciousness that she recognizes that writing alone will not solve the African's crisis. Tactically, she employs her novels as vehicles to incite action. They are, in fact, social and political treatises; not simply aesthetically pleasing, but, in making a social statement, they are didactic because she understands the urgency of arriving at a solution for the African's crisis. She states that "if the race is to survive, it has to take care of its own."[19] Her unobscured understanding of this fact determines the purpose of her writing. In alluding to Song of Solomon, Susan Willis astutely writes that the characters' struggle "to reclaim or redefine themselves" results from their understanding that "it is the strength and continuity of the black cultural heritage as a whole which is at stake."[20] Then, too, just as Morrison makes her characters struggle, she strives to make her readers struggle. According to Willis, "Morrison writes to awaken her reader's sensitivity, to shake up and disrupt the sensual numbing that accompanies social and psychological alienation."[21] Simply stated, Morrison's purpose is to use her novels as tools to politically educate her readers about their race oppression and class exploitation and, by doing so, to stimulate them to rejuvenate themselves in the true spirit of the new African personality, one that has the positive elements of traditional Africa as its core.[22]

One of her most predominant and successful methods of politically educating her readers is her practice of juxtaposing the negative elements of capitalist societies with the positive elements of the traditional African way of life. In doing so, Morrison reveals the inherent injustices of capitalism and, as a consequence, encourages her audience to embrace those positive elements of traditional Africa. In all of her novels, she incorporates the African principles of collectivism, humanism, and egalitarianism. Collectivism is the idea that individual development is conditioned by group development—the responsibility of the many for each. According to this principle, the welfare of the people, not the individual, is supreme. The traditional African concept of humanism regards the person "as primarily a spiritual being, a being endowed originally with a certain dignity, integrity and value."[23] He or she is seen, in effect, as an end in himself or herself, not as a means to an end. The principle of egalitarianism signifies the duty and the right of the individual to work to transform his or her environment and to receive the just rewards for this service.

The incorporation of these principles in Morrison's works is pointed out by several critics as well as by the author herself. In regard to the concept of collectivism, for example, Barbara Christian writes that Morrison's worlds "are very much like villages" with their emphasis on kinship.[24] In an interview with Judith Wilson, Morrison emphasizes the need for the whole village to raise a child, and in an interview with Robert E. Stepto, she speaks of the value of the neighborhood and equates it with the traditional concept of the "compound" within the African village.[25]

An additional successful method of politically educating African people utilized by Morrison is her knack for making African culture in toto come alive. The incorporation of superstition, numerology, omens, herbal remedies, natural imagery, the art of naming, and language patterns such as call and response are Africanisms that imbue her work and confirm her commitment to struggle.

A number of critics have astutely observed some of the thematic similarities in Morrison's canon, and a few have remarked on the development of her canon, but none have connected the similarities with the advancement of her theme and structure; none have conducted a careful study of this developing canon; none have seen this advancement as Morrison's struggle to arrive at a solution for the African's plight; and none have connected this advancement to Morrison's own developing class consciousness. Barbara Christian, for instance, remarks that "there is a consistency of vision in [Morrison's first] three novels, for they focus on the seemingly contradictory urges of human beings to be a part of Nature, yet distinct from it."[26] In a later essay, this same critic writes about Morrison's development of the class concept within her canon but does not examine this development in connection with Morrison's own heightened consciousness.[27] Jacqueline DeWeever indirectly alludes to Morrison's literary development when she states that "*The Bluest Eyes* ends with Pecola's madness at twelve years old, when she has entered maturity; *Sula* begins with the story of Shadrack's madness."[28] Grace Ann Hovet comments that "across her [first] three novels, Morrison's characters are generally divided into three kinds of fliers."[29]

Perhaps more than any other critic, Julie Nichols comes close to observing the thematic and structural patterns in Morrison's canon. Nichols writes: "When I read *Tar Baby* (1981) and searched out her earlier *Sula* (1973), I was impressed by the patterns in all three novels [including *Song of Solomon*] and with their individual and cumulative effects."[30] Other than making this perceptive observation, however, Nichols gives no impressive evidence of these patterns. Instead, she ends her article with the stated desire "to teach all three novels to an entire class" and to have the class project Morrison's "next novel's plot and structure, theme and images."[31]

Clearly, there is thematic and structural development found in Morrison's works. Morrison uses each novel as a framework for investigating various solutions to the African's dilemma. Each successive novel reflects her growing understanding of what the solution cannot be (the destruction of racism and sexism) and, thus, like a scientist she moves closer to discovering what it can be (the destruction of capitalism).

Dialectically, as she investigates the nature of the African's oppression through her primary theme—the search for identity—her narrative structure develops as well. She learns to artistically shape her theme so as to provide accurate presentations without the aid of artificial props and gimmicks. Moreover, these presentations become more and more collectivized, reflecting her growing consciousness of the negativity of that selfish, devil-may-care individualism promoted by capitalism.

A brief description of the interrelationship between theme and structure in the Morrisonian canon will prove valuable at this point. *The Bluest Eye* reveals the extent of the crisis of the African personality when an African child born in the United States falls prey to the teachings of the dominant society. Believing that she is an ugly "black e mo," Pecola Breedlove thinks that having the blue eyes of Shirley Temple will make her beautiful and lovable. While class oppression, the primary cause of the African's oppression, is treated in the novel, it is overshadowed by Morrison's emphasis on racism. Just as the theme of *The Bluest Eye* is unnatural in its limited focus on the African's dilemma, so the structure is inchoate, relying on external gimmicks such as the inclusion/omission of storybook-passage headings to help develop the theme. Overall, the structure is like a puzzle, enigmatic and difficult to piece together.

In *Sula*, Morrison grapples with the idea of individual or gender freedom as the African's solution: the answer to Sula's dilemma of being born "black and female" seems to lie in her simply rejecting the traditional role ascribed to women and becoming an artist. Clearly, Morrison's investigation of equal opportunities for women is a logical next step after her examination of racism in *The Bluest Eye*. *Sula*, in effect, takes up where *The Bluest Eye* leaves off: when *Sula* opens, the heroine is the twelve-year-old Pecola, isolated and oppressed. Nevertheless, Morrison's belief that the primary cause of Sula's demise is gender oppression is incorrect and the solution—becoming an artist—a reflection of the author's own immature consciousness. Morrison, and thus her protagonists of later novels, will come to understand that sexism and racism can only exist and blossom in a society that is inherently unjust, one based on the profitable exploitation of humankind, and one that, as a consequence, sets up notions of inferiority and superiority. Such an understanding of capitalism is reflected to some extent in *Sula*, but it too is overshadowed by Morrison's stress on the gender oppression of women.

Like that of *The Bluest Eye*, the structure of *Sula* is artificial, yet it does demonstrate Morrison's growing confidence in her writing ability, a confidence that to some extent must be credited to her increasing awareness of the plight of African people. Certainly, it is a development over the structure of *The Bluest Eye*. For example, instead of relying on passage headings and an introductory page filled with a quote from the Dick and Jane primary reader, Morrison relies only on a short passage from the "Rose Tattoo" and dates to develop the storyline of *Sula*. By doing so, she is forced to rely on her own storytelling ability.

Song of Solomon reflects a qualitative leap forward in Morrison's growing consciousness, for she understands that the African in the United States suffers equally from race and class oppression. Thus, in this novel, the protagonist realizes that to overcome his crisis he must first understand how he became crisis-ridden. He must know his history, knowledge that will awaken him to the common plight of African people. Milkman Dead, as a consequence, learns to identify with the African masses, not, like Sula, to distinguish himself from them. However, while such a realization and an identification are valuable, they are not enough. Milkman must understand that his awareness of the common oppression of African people as manifested in their history and in their present is relevant only if it is used to struggle against the cause of that oppression. Both knowledge and commitment are needed.

Song of Solomon is free of the structural props that the novice writer relies on to help her tell her story. Morrison is mature enough to recognize the benefit of allowing a story to grow without external, obtrusive introductions and chapter headings, just as a people must be allowed to grow without external interference.

Tar Baby is an assimilation and advancement of the primary theme of her three earlier novels. For the first time, Morrison frees her work from the narrow geographical boundaries of American society. Recognizing that people of African descent, no matter where they live, share a common identity, a common history, and a common oppression, she uses an island in the Caribbean as the dominant and pivotal setting for her novel. In doing so, Morrison reflects her own maturing consciousness of the fact that African people must seek a common solution to their plight. She herself states that "Black culture survives everywhere pretty much the same" and that "Black people take their culture wherever they go."[32]

Furthermore, in *Tar Baby* Morrison creates a revolutionary protagonist, Son, who realizes that he cannot run away and leave a body. Having discovered first the importance of knowing one's history and one's relationship to his people, Son commits himself to sharing this knowledge with other Africans. Thus, by struggling to politically educate Therese, Gideon, Sydney, Ondine, and, in particular, Jadine—symbols of the larger Pan-African society—Son becomes a disciple for African people, a modern-day revolutionary. Unfortunately, although his goal is a noble one, indeed Christ-like, his solution of a return to a traditional lifestyle is based on idealism, rather than Nkrumaism. If we accept the Nkrumaist view that everything develops to some higher state and that African people have their own particular history and culture, "Then African thought in the mid-20th century cannot escape powerful influences which have permeated" the African's psyche.[33] Moreover, what Son fails to realize is that there are some Africans, like Jadine, who—because they share the aspirations of the ruling class and receive handouts from it—

will refuse to struggle against capitalism even though they are conscious of the fact that it is the primary enemy of African people.

Despite its weaknesses, the novel's theme and narrative structure reflect Morrison's heightened class consciousness. Structurally, she has embraced the traditional African concept of collectivism, for each of the major characters, as well as the omniscient narrator, contributes to the organic world of the novel. The story is told, in effect, by taking individual threads and sewing them into a whole, a wholeness that she so ardently wishes for African people.

After reading the first four novels as evolutionary, the Morrisonian critic becomes convinced of the author's knack for self-criticism, her habit of reexamining earlier theories and assumptions. Thus, it is reasonable for the critic to think that Morrison's next novel would examine, as a solution to the African's crisis, the African's collectivized struggle against capitalism. *Beloved* does just that. It examines a critical historical period in the African's life in order primarily to demonstrate that African people have and thus can survive the most oppressive conditions by collectively struggling against them. Structurally, in her efforts to juxtapose what was done with what can be done, Toni Morrison manipulates time by continually jettisoning the reader back and forth from past to present. Surely, the message is that if it was done before, it can be done again. African people can survive their present day crisis through organization. A worthwhile message indeed.

2
The Bluest Eye
The Need for Racial Approbation

In The Bluest Eye, Toni Morrison's emphasis is on racism. Specifically, she investigates the effects of the beauty standards of the dominant culture on the self-image of the African female adolescent. The role of class, the primary form of exploitation experienced by African people that will become the focus of later works, is only relevant insofar as it exacerbates that self-image. Of the three main characters—all African female adolescents—it is Pecola Breedlove who is the primary focus. It is she who is most affected by the dominant culture's beauty standards because it is she who is the poorest and, consequently, the most vulnerable. Thus, even with this early work, Morrison is conscious of the role economics plays in the African's having a wholesome self-image. For it is the Breedloves' fight for survival that weakens the family structure and makes the family members more vulnerable to the propaganda of the dominant culture. Still, it is clear that in The Bluest Eye Morrison regards racism as the African's primary obstacle. Describing the Breedloves, she writes: "Although their poverty was traditional and stultifying, it was not unique. But their ugliness was unique."[1] This comment demonstrates that in the late 1960s, when this novel was written, Morrison's level of consciousness about the primary cause of the nature of the African's oppression in the United States as well as in the rest of the world was considerably weak, for she not only subordinates the role of economics to racism, but also neglects to show a causal relationship between them, that an exploitive economic system gives rise to racist ideology.

The thesis of the novel is that racism devastates the self-image of the African female in general and the African female child in particular.[2] Toni Morrison's emphasis is on the society, not the family unit. According to her, the African's self-image is destroyed at an early age as a result of the ruling class's (i.e., the European capitalist class's) promotion of its own standard of beauty: long, stringy hair, preferably blond; keen nose, thin lips; and light eyes, preferably blue. By analogy, if the physical features of the European are accepted as the standard of beauty, then the African must be ugly. This is the type of logic that the Breedloves use to convince themselves of their ugliness:

> They had looked about themselves and saw nothing to contradict the statement; saw, in fact, support for it leaning at them from every billboard, every movie, every glance. "Yes," they had said. "You are right." And they took the ugliness in their hands, threw it as a mantle over them, and went about the world with it.[3]

Although Morrison clearly and correctly understands that the concept of beauty is a learned one—Claudia MacTeer learns to love the big, blue-eyed baby doll she is given for Christmas; Maureen Peal learns she is beautiful from the propaganda of the dominant society as well as from the African adult world; and Pauline Breedlove learns from the silver screen that every face must be assigned some category on the scale of absolute beauty— Morrison does not yet understand that this concept will change depending on the racial makeup of the dominant class. That is, her immature class consciousness at this point in her writing career precludes her understanding of three important facts: first, that the ruling class, whether of European, African, or Asian descent, possesses the major instruments of economic production and distribution as well as the means of establishing its socio-cultural dominance (i.e., all forms of media including books, billboards, and movies); second, that possessing such means, the ruling class uses and promotes its own image as a measurement of beauty for the entire society; and third, that the success of this promotion ensures the continual dominance of this ruling class.

Although her class analysis is immature at this point, Morrison is at least conscious of a limited role that economics plays in the exploitation of African people. For example, Morrison begins *The Bluest Eye* with a page and a half of one passage repeated in three different ways. Each of the passages reflects the three primary families in the novel: the Dick-Jane primary reader family, the MacTeer family, and the Breedlove family. The first family is symbolic of the ruling class; it is an economically stable family. Both the MacTeers and the Breedloves symbolize the exploited class although the Breedloves are less economically stable than the MacTeers. In fact, the spacing of the passages reflects the varying economic levels of these families. Although the Mac-Teers are poor, the father works and provides some shelter, food, and clothing for the economic survival of the family. On the other hand, the Breedloves are dirt poor, and it is the extent of their poverty that strips them of their sense of human worth and leaves them more vulnerable to the cultural propaganda of the ruling class. Their house, significantly a run-down, abandoned store, reflects no stability. The family members come and go like store patrons, having no sense of family love and unity. That Morrison takes the time to describe and explain the poor economic conditions of the Breedlove family, and the effects of these conditions on it, reflects her awareness of the class question. At least she informs the reader that the MacTeers and Breedloves do not suffer simply because of racism, but because of poverty as well.

Additionally, Morrison reveals her class consciousness by exploring the intraracial prejudices caused by petty bourgeois Africans, those who aspire for the same goals and aspirations of the ruling class. In *The Bluest Eye*, she creates three "minor" African families who, because they benefit economically, politically, and/ or socially from the exploitation of their own people, disassociate themselves from poor Africans and associate themselves with the ruling class.

One such family is the Peals. Although the reader is introduced to only one member of this family, Maureen, her appearance, behavioral patterns, and remarks about the nature of her family's "business" offer sufficient glimpses of the Peals to reflect their class interests. Physically, Maureen looks and dresses like a little European-American girl, the storybook Jane or the child actress Shirley Temple. Her hairstyle, "long brown hair braided into two lynch ropes that hung down her back" resembles that of little European girls. In fact, the description of her hair as lynch ropes clearly associates her with the African's oppressors.[4] Her "high-yellow" complexion and her clothes make this association even more pronounced. She wears "Kelly-green knee socks," "lemon-drop sweaters," "brown velvet coat trimmed in white rabbit fur, and a matching muff."[5]

Socially, Maureen's behavior patterns reflect the way in which some within the dominant class relate to poor African people. She pities Pecola when she is humiliated by Bay Boy and Junie Bug, and she humors Claudia by speaking to her on one occasion after neglecting her on many others. Economically, the Peal family appears to make money by exploiting the race issue. They initiate suits against European-American establishments (e.g., Isaley's ice cream store in Akron) that refuse to serve Africans. Although, according to Maureen, her "family does it all the time,"[6] apparently these suits are benefitting financially no other African family but the Peals.

Still, Morrison is more interested in developing the skin-color conflict (race) than the class conflict (capitalism). For the emphasis in the Peal section is on "unearned haughtiness," Maureen's physical appearance. She looks like the doll that Claudia has had to learn to love; she is the person whom the teachers smile at encouragingly, the parents talk to in honey-coated voices, the boys leave alone; she is Shirley Temple; she is Jane. Moreover, Maureen's last appearance in the novel is clearly associated with the question of intraracial prejudice based on skin color. When Maureen is verbally attacked by Claudia, she responds by using the same dehumanizing name calling that Bay Boy used against Pecola: "I *am* cute! And you ugly! Black and ugly black e mos. I *am* cute!"[7] Clearly, Maureen sees herself as superior because she looks more like her oppressors.[8]

By disassociating itself from the African community, the second family—Geraldine, Louis, and Louis Junior—also reflects ruling class aspirations. The family members consider themselves to be *colored*, a term that for them signifies some nebulous group of Africans who are neither European nor African: "Colored people were neat and quiet; niggers were dirty and loud."[9] So Louis Jr. plays with European-American children; his hair is cut short to deemphasize its woolliness; his skin is continually lotioned to keep him from revealing his ashy Africanness. When Geraldine sees Pecola, she is reminded of everything she has sought to escape—everything associated with the poor, struggling African masses: their physical appearance, their behavioral patterns, their lifestyle, and their speech patterns. Her calling

Pecola, a little girl of ten, a "nasty little black bitch" and com-
manding her to "get out of my house" illustrate the extent of
Geraldine's isolation from her people and her association with
her oppressors. Perhaps even more significant is the fact that she
showers love on her black cat, but not her "black" son. Clearly,
for her, the blue eyes of the cat make it easier to love the animal
than her own son. All in all, her thoughts, words, and actions
parrot those of the ruling class.

The third family, the Elihue Micah Whitcombs, are so obsessed
with the physical appearance of Europeans that they jeopardize
their mental stability by intermarrying to maintain some sem-
blance of whiteness. They are grateful that their ancestor, a de-
caying British nobleman, chose to whiten them, and they
enthusiastically separate themselves "in body, mind, and spirit
from all that suggested Africa" while developing "Anglo-
philia."[10] They are, in fact, convinced of DeGobineau's hypothesis that "all civilizations derive from the white race, that none
can exist without its help, and that a great society is great and
brilliant only so far as it preserves the blood of the noble group
that created it."[11] Not only do the Whitcombs strive for the
"whiteness" of the ruling class, but they imitate the exploitive
nature of this class as well; they exploit their own people, the
Africans who live in the West Indies: "That they were corrupt in
public and private practice, both lecherous and lascivious, was
considered their noble right."[12]

Clearly, Morrison's class consciousness, however weak, is reflected in her condemnation of these families who share the class
aspirations of their oppressors. All suffer from what Kwame
Nkrumah called the crisis of the African personality—Africans
so bereft of their own national identity that they exhibit distorted, even psychopathic, behavioral patterns. Morrison is certainly aware of this crisis, for in this work as in later ones, she
harshly criticizes those characters who divorce themselves from
the African community. In fact, she considers this petty bourgeois sector of the African population the living dead, a buffer
group between the ruling and the oppressed classes who are
always portrayed as abnormal in some sense. In *The Bluest Eye*,
Geraldine lavishes love on her black cat, but withholds it from
her son; the Whitcombs become a family of morons and perverts.
Quite appropriately, Elihue is donned Soaphead Wilson by the

community for he is a pervert who is incapable of healthy love. Instead, he loves worn things and little girls; Pecola is both worn (loss of virginity) and a little girl.

Morrison's characterization of these three "minor" families—the Peals, the "Geraldines," and the Whitcombs—certainly substantiates the premise that she does possess some class consciousness even in this first novel. However, that these are not major families in the novel indicates that her class consciousness is decidedly weak. Moreover, even though Morrison is conscious of the role class aspirations play in these minor families, she often discusses these aspirations as if they were intraracial prejudices based on skin color rather than class conflicts. That is, her discussions of class conflicts are couched within, and thus overshadowed by, her discussions on racial prejudices. Indeed, it is interesting to note that just as Africans in the United States in the 1960s and early 1970s viewed the primary enemy of African people as "the white man," so does Morrison, writing *The Bluest Eye* in the late 1960s, see the issue as one of European versus African. However, as she continues to think about, write about, and experience the ongoing oppression of African people despite the gains of the Civil Rights Movement, she will become more conscious of the fact that capitalism, not racism, is the African's greatest enemy.

It is interesting to surmise that the limited focus on the issue of class as the primary problem confronting African people in *The Bluest Eye* and the primary focus on racism as the major concern may be dialectically related to the novel's inorganic structure. The structural limitations of the novel can be gleened through the many artificial props that Morrison relies on to help her develop her theme. First, she includes two prefaces, one to inform the reader of the conflict in the novel, the other to present the outcome. The first preface, extracted from the Dick-Jane primary reader, presents the three dominant families that will be contrasted in the novel: the Dick-Jane family, the MacTeers, and the Breedloves. Each is represented by one of the three storybook passages that Morrison places at the beginning of the novel to give the reader his or her first clue as to the economic and social well-being—or lack thereof—of the families. The structure of the first passage, representing the Dick-Jane household, is correct according to the double spacing and punctuation requirements of a standard typewritten passage. The next passage lacks the traditional structure of the first. It is single spaced. Representing the MacTeer household, it signifies neither the ideal nor complete chaos. Rather, it reflects a struggling household, one that manages to survive despite its economic hardships. The third passage is completely devoid of spacing and punctuation. Its words are run together, reflecting the chaos found in the Breedlove household. Therefore, just as the second two passages are presented to enable the reader to compare and contrast them with the first, so the MacTeer and Breedlove families are presented to enable the reader to compare and contrast their condition in society with that of the standard or ideal European-American family, the Dick-Jane family. The structural layout of the passages enhances the theme that as Africans born in a racist society, neither the MacTeers nor the Breedloves enjoy the benefits of America that their European counterparts do.

The second preface, the marigold page, presents the outcome of the novel—the unfortunate and irreparable demise of Pecola Breedlove in particular and of the Breedlove family in general. It also reveals the reason for this demise; the infertile soil of Lorain, Ohio, symbolic of the United States, precludes the healthy, normal growth of the marigolds, symbolic of African-American people.

Another prop used by Morrison to help her tell her story is the use of three different levels of time. First, the reader is introduced to a present that exists outside of the novel proper, the present of the adult Claudia. Second, the reader is given a glimpse of the future within the context of the novel, the marigold preface. Third, the story proper actually begins in the present on page twelve. However, by page seventeen, with the introduction of Pecola, and certainly by page thirty, with the description of the Breedlove's store house, the reader does not know what time period exists. Does Pecola come to live with the MacTeers after the Breedlove's abandoned store house is burned, or does Cholly burn some other, prior dwelling place, and then the Breedloves move into the abandoned store? Such questions arise because of Morrison's clumsy handling of time throughout the novel. She is not yet skilled in structuring plots.

The use of names of seasons to indicate the major parts of the novel also aids Morrison in telling her story. By beginning the novel with autumn, she informs us that the world of the novel is topsy turvey. Spring usually symbolizes the beginning of things, the time of birth and rebirth. Autumn, in contrast, is the time of death and decay. Summer, commonly associated with life in full bloom, ripeness, is a time of death, life in its final moments. These seasonal divisions aid the reader in understanding the fundamental decadence of life for the African living in the United States. They help tell Morrison's story of the warped psyche of an adolescent African female living in a racist society.[13]

A fourth structural crutch is Morrison's reliance on a series of passage chapter headings primarily to let the reader know that the Breedlove family will be the focus of the chapters and, secondarily, to let the reader know what specific aspect of the family will be the focus. For example, chapter 2, the first section that concerns the Breedloves, has as its heading a run-together passage describing the house of Dick and Jane. By using this particular passage as the heading, Morrison informs the reader that the contents of the chapter will be devoted to a description of the Breedlove house. When a heading includes all the members of the Dick-Jane family, as in chapter 3, the reader knows that all the Breedloves will be discussed. Admittedly, Morrison has created an interesting and unique structural device. Still, these headings do in fact simplify her task as a writer, for she can rely on them to help organize her material, i.e., to help develop the plot of *The Bluest Eye*. In later works, such devices are omitted because they are unnecessary. Moreover, they distract the reader from concentrating on the narrative itself. In later works, Morrison demonstrates her developed consciousness, her developed writing ability, and her developed confidence by relying only on the narrative to tell her story. In other words, the act of writing itself helps her class consciousness develop, and her developed class consciousness enhances her writing skills. The two are dialectically related.

Morrison's reliance on three narrators—Claudia the child, Claudia the adult, and an omniscient narrator—is problematic as well.[14] For instance, as narrator, Claudia the adult at times ascribes her adult feelings and adult analytical ability to Claudia the child. The reader is amazed, for instance, that a nine-year-old can understand that U.S. capitalist society is to blame for creating the standard of beauty: "And all the time we knew that Maureen Peal was not the Enemy and not worthy of such intense hatred. The *Thing* to fear was the *Thing* that made her beautiful, and not us."[15] For most, this realization does not come until adulthood. Phyllis Klotman attempts to offer a logical explanation for this shift in point of view from the child to the adult Claudia when she writes: "The narrative voice shifts . . . when the author wants us to have a more mature and objective view of the characters and their situations. . . . There is not only a progression in Claudia's point of view from youth to age, but also from ignorance to perception."[16] Contrarily, Morrison's narrative structure is more illogical than logical since Claudia the child thinks like an adult at times and a child at others. There is not what Klotman refers to as "a progression in Claudia's point of view." Throughout the novel, the reader constantly asks the following question: Is Claudia, the adult narrator, looking back on her childhood and telling the story, or is she telling the story as a nine-year-old participant and an adult observer?

The use of the omniscient narrator adds to this narrative confusion and awkwardness. It is the omniscient narrator who tells the Breedlove's story; Claudia, the child and/or adult, relates the events within the remaining chapters. What prevents the reader from being totally confused by this arrangement is the inclusion or omission of chapter headings. Chapters without headings are told by Claudia; those with headings are told by the omniscient narrator. However, this understanding of Morrison's narrative structure does not rid it of its awkwardness. On the contrary, the division of the story in such a way contributes to the reader's impression that Morrison, at this early stage in her writing career, must rely on artificial or external textural devices to organize her material.

Just as there are organization weaknesses between chapters, so are there weaknesses within chapters. In interviews with both Jane Bakerman and Robert Stepto, Morrison admits that she had difficulty with the Pauline Breedlove section of the novel. Unable to have either of her three narrators—the omniscient narrator, the adult Claudia, or the child Claudia—tell Pauline's story, Morrison is forced to use italics to symbolize Mrs. Breedlove's own thoughts. Morrison admits this writing weakness to Bakerman:

When I wrote the section in *The Bluest Eye* about Pecola's mother, I thought I would have no trouble. First I wrote it out as an "I" story, . . . then I wrote it out as a "she" story. . . . I was never able to resolve that, so I used both. The author said a little bit and then she said a little bit. But I wish I had been able to do the "I" thing with her. I really wanted to.[17]

To Robert Stepto, she says: "I sort of copped out . . . because I used two voices."[18]

Having to oscillate between Pauline's thoughts within italics and the omniscient narrator's comments within a single chapter is only one instance of Morrison's inability to make her text cohere. The introduction of Pecola is another. At the end of one paragraph, Morrison completes a discussion of Mr. Henry Washington, the MacTeer's new boarder. At the beginning of the next, Pecola is introduced by the following nebulous statement: "She slept in the bed with us."[19] There is no transition from the discussion on Mr. Henry to that on Pecola. Neither is there a legitimate stylistic reason for this textual gap since for the reader it creates confusion, not clarity.

Too, there is at least one chapter—the Geraldine-Junior chapter—that seems superfluous to the rest of the text because it is not clearly integrated with the other chapters. Unlike the Maureen Peal section, which clearly helps to explain the effects of racism within the African race, and unlike the Soaphead Wilson section, which is relevant in providing the conditions under which Pecola imagines she has blue eyes, the Geraldine-Junior section seemingly does not advance the plot of *The Bluest Eye*. At first glance, it appears merely as a repetition of an already established fact: Pecola has an all-consuming desire to have blue eyes. However, it actually moves beyond repetition by relating the circumstances under which Pecola becomes convinced that she can be "black" and have blue eyes and, by convincing her of this fact, helps to seal her fate. But for Morrison to use an entire chapter to make this point (and then to make it so unclearly) is a mark of her undeveloped writing skills.

Later works evidence a symbiosis between text and structure, for as Morrison better understands capitalism/imperialism—the exploitation of one class of people by another class—she will structure her text to represent the type of economic system that condemns exploitation and promotes collectivism: socialism. Thus, by the time she writes *Tar Baby*, her story will be told equally by all of the main characters in the novel as well as by the omniscient narrator. Each will have the opportunity and the responsibility to contribute to the organic whole. And by the time she writes *Beloved*, she will so expertly manipulate past, present, and future as to demonstrate to African people that there is no significant difference between the quality of their life now and that experienced in slavery. This devotion to creating a dialectical relationship between text and structure will, in turn, point the way to the solution: collectivism.

3
Sula
The Struggle for Individual Fulfillment

As the introductory quote from *The Rose Tattoo* suggests, in *Sula* Toni Morrison is more interested in the struggle for individual rights in general and women's rights in particular than with the rights of African people as a collective. The quote is especially interesting when juxtaposed with the introductory pages of *The Bluest Eyes*. The lines "Nobody knew my rose of the world but me. . . . I had too much glory" connote the plight of the individual who is at odds with society. In contrast, the Dick and Jane passages that frame Morrison's first novel stress the African people's struggle against racism in the United States. Interestingly enough, the thematic thrust of each novel chronicles the historical struggle of African people: The sixties marked the Civil Rights Struggle; the seventies emphasized rights for the individual, in particular the woman. The latter was a consequence of the former, for out of the struggle for civil rights came an awareness of self, and dignity and pride in self. Unfortunately, during the time she was writing *Sula*, Morrison made the same mistake as did many Africans: She wrote about these struggles as if they were independent and unrelated episodes, rather than steps, in the African's struggle for equality, and she saw them as causes, rather than effects, of the African's oppression in the United States. Thus, with *Sula* as with *The Bluest Eye*, sex, race, and class oppression are explored; however, the primacy of each changes. It is not until her fourth novel, *Tar Baby*, that the question of class as it relates to capitalism is investigated as a primary theme.

Morrison's weak class analysis at the time she writes *Sula* forces her to create a female character who, because of her oppression, makes individualism supreme over the collective, rather than a female character who struggles to change the oppressive nature of society in order to ensure the full development of each individual, whether male or female. In the words of Karen Stein, in *Sula*, "The truest heroism lies not in external battle, as in the wars which destroy the novel's men, but in confrontation with the self."[1] Indeed, Morrison's weak analysis precludes her understanding of the symbiosis that exists between the individual and the group: Individuality is rewarding only if it is achieved within the context of the community well-being. Sula struggles for a niche of her own, unconscious or unmindful of the fact that the free development of each is conditioned by the free development of all.

The oppression of African women in the United States, especially in the first quarter of the twentieth century, is documented throughout the novel. Morrison's most articulate statement in regard to the female's degradation comes in a passage that appears after Nel and Sula first meet: "Because each had discovered years before they were neither white nor male, and that all freedom and triumph was forbidden to them, they had set about creating something else to be."[2] Within this statement are found both the dilemma of the novel and the solution to the dilemma: African women are oppressed, and to escape their oppression, they must become self-propagators. Accordingly, Sula rejects the traditional role ascribed to women, telling Eva, "I want to make myself."[3] However, since her oppression as a woman is the result of an oppressive economic system, not men, Sula finds it impossible to escape all of the traditionalisms associated with women. When she becomes intimately involved with Ajax, she discovers, for example, that she knows no other postures other than the ones traditionally associated with women who are in love: feminine meekness, "prettiness," and possessiveness. In fact, no others are nurtured by the society. Thus, to escape, to recreate self within the context of this novel, Sula has only two options: to become a "man" or to die. She chooses death.[4]

The manner in which Morrison chooses to explore the nature of the woman's oppression is unique. She develops two female characters, neither of whom is complete in herself. Although Morrison does not yet demonstrate full consciousness of the facts that the full human development of a woman is precluded under capitalism and that to be fully, wholesomely developed her characters must come together as one, these facts seem to be embedded in her subconscious. Interviewed by Jane Bakerman, Morrison states: "If they were one woman, they would be complete."[5] As they are, Nel and Sula represent two extremes; their surnames are indicative of each. In Nel Wright's household, too many directions are given: Nel's house is "incredibly orderly."[6] In Sula Peace's household, none are given: "It is a household of throbbing disorder."[7] To be right (Wright) means to follow the path that has been laid out for you by society; to be at peace is to be left alone to pursue whatever path you wish. Thus, "the two of them together," according to Morrison, "could have made a wonderful single human being."[8]

This idea that Nel and Sula represent two halves of one person reverberates throughout the novel. As children, they often decide to perform some act or play some game "in concert, without ever meeting each other's eyes."[9] Eva, in response to Nel's shocked reaction to being called Sula, says: "You. Sula. What's the difference?"[10] When Sula returns to the Bottom, Nel thinks that her friend's return "was like getting an eye back" and that talking to Sula "had always been a conversation with herself."[11] Significant too is Morrison's statement: "Their friendship was so close, they themselves had difficulty distinguishing one's thoughts from the other's."[12] Perhaps what is most insightful is the parcticular halves that each represents: Sula, the mind; Nel, the body. Nel's mind dies when Sula leaves Medallion, but her body continues to perform the routine, necessary chores traditionally associated with women. In contrast, Sula's mind continues to function after her body ceases to do so: "Well, I'll be damned . . . it [death] didn't even hurt. Wait'll I tell Nel."[13]

Her status as only one half person launches Sula on a quest to become whole. She rejects Eva's advice of settling down and having babies, replying, "I don't want to make somebody else. I want to make myself."[14] But because Sula's struggle to enjoy her fullest potential as a human being is a struggle waged against the Bottom community instead of capitalism, she struggles alone and unsuccessfully. Unfortunately, she does not connect her oppression with the oppression of the entire community. And without such a connection, her struggle is doomed.[15]

Interestingly enough, although Sula is like Shadrack—they are both pariahs—her goal is at variance with his. Both recognize the

oppressive plight of African people caused by the dominant
society. However, their solutions to that plight are quite different.
Shadrack, who has "no past, no language, no tribe, no source,"
longs for a place in the community.[16] It is both his longing for a
viable existence within the community and his recognition of the
need for collective struggle against the oppressive forces of the
society as a prerequisite for that existence that cause him to
create National Suicide Day. On the third day of January of every
year, Shadrack, leading a parade of African people, marches
through the Bottom. It is on this day that Africans are supposed
to demonstrate their commitment to life and their defiance of
death. And life, for Shadrack as well as Sula, does not mean
submitting to oppression but forging a wholesome life even if it
means confronting death.

On the other hand, Sula, who has "no center, no speck around
which to grow,"[17] longs for a "postcoital privateness" in which
she can join "herself in matchless harmony."[18] Not realizing the
dialectical relationship between the collective and individual
interests, Sula ultimately betrays and alienates family, friends,
and neighbors, thereby causing her own death. Ranking her particular individualism supreme above all else, she unemotionally
watches her mother burn to death, seduces her best friend's
husband, and places her grandmother in a nursing home. She
becomes a pariah, living outside the laws and mores of the
community. As Nel attests, "Talking to her about right and wrong
was like talking to the deweys."[19]

When Sula returns to the Bottom after a ten-year absence, she
is accompanied by a plague of robins that shit all over the community and then die. Sula too shits on the Bottom community
and dies. Through a series of thoughtless, cruel acts committed
against the community, she will be perceived as its enemy, "The
source of their personal misfortune."[20] Her casual sexual relationships with the men of the Bottom, unlike Hannah's, emascu-
late them and insult the women: "She would lay their hus-
bands once and then no more. . . . Sula was trying them and
discarding them without any excuse the men could swallow."[21]
She attends the community's church suppers without underwear
and, so the community thinks, sleeps with white men—the most
filthy act in which any African woman can engage. By the time
Sula dies, she is completely isolated from the community: she is

confined in Eva's boarded up room, symbolizing that a person outside of the collective is like a head cut off from a body; she is visited by no one except Nel, on one occasion; and, after death, she is prepared for burial by white folks, since no one in the community would "do" for her. Interestingly, her rose-shaped birthmark symbolizes her increasing degradation and isolation. In the mold of *The Picture of Dorian Gray*, Sula's birthmark darkens with each successive violation of the community's taboos. Significantly, when she sees Sula after ten years, Nel thinks that her friend's birthmark is darker than Nel remembered.[22]

In accordance with the principles of dialectics, the consequence of Sula's thoughtless, often cruel, acts against her people have both negative and positive effects. Although these acts anger and frighten the community, causing them to lay broomsticks across their doors at night and sprinkle salt on their steps, they see in Sula someone against whom they can unite; they "band together against the devil in their midst."[23] Betty, Teapot's mother, becomes a better parent, "sober, clean and industrious";[24] the women "cherish their men more";[25] and the community begins to love one another.[26] Despite these positive effects, the community perceives Sula as the enemy, a perception that is incorrect. Barbara Christian agrees: "Rather than focusing its attention on the pervasive evils of racism and poverty that continually threaten it, the community expends its energy on outlasting the evil Sula."[27] The enemy is the society, not Sula, not men, not the Bottom community. It is the world of the novel—a microcosm of the United States—that conditions the thinking of, indeed, creates Sula, the men, and the community.

All of them—Sula, the Bottom community, and Morrison herself—seem to come to this realization of who the enemy is, or at least who it is not, by the end of the novel. However, for each this awareness seems to be in embryo form. For instance, Sula's last words reflect a surprised recognition of her need for the community, since her address to Nel represents Sula's need of the Other: " 'Well, I'll be damned,' she thought, 'it didn't even hurt. Wait'll I tell Nel.' "[28] By admitting her need for this Other, Sula helps to redeem herself. The community is not her enemy, but her much needed friend. Then, too, the community instinctively marches to the New River Road, a place associated with the Europeans' broken promise of jobs for the Africans of Medallion.

By its actions, the community acknowledges its perception of Europeans, not Sula, as its enemy. And by presenting no viable solution for the individual African's struggle for freedom—Sula can neither survive without the community nor fly away and leave it—Morrison unconsciously points to society as the enemy.

While it is true that the African people's struggle for individual freedom is the primary focus of *Sula*, it is also true that African people's struggle for national freedom is a secondary focus. Issues of race are interwoven throughout the fabric of the novel. Having its basis in racism and having its roots in slavery, the origin of the Bottom is the novel's starting point. When a slavemaster gives hilly land instead of the promised fertile valley land to his faithful slave, the slave "blinked and said he thought valley land was bottom land. The master said, 'Oh, no! . . . That's bottom land, rich and fertile. . . . It's the bottom of heaven—the best land there is.' "[29] Once again, it is the Europeans who decide the destiny of African people, in this case by misnaming.

The deweys' lack of development is another example of racism. Each of the deweys has physical characteristics completely distinct from the others. Yet they appear to look alike, reminding the reader of the stereotype, "All niggers look alike," and they never never grow, suggesting that living in a racist society thwarts the natural development of African people. Also, Tar Baby's and Ajax's arrest symbolizes just one more incident in which African people or anyone associated with them are routinely arrested and beaten. Ajax calls this cycle of oppression "the natural hazards of Negro life."[30] Finally, the events surrounding and following National Suicide Day (1941) are racially motivated.

Frustrated by their exploitation and hopeful of a better life, the community, in January 1941, participates in this annual event for the first time:

> The same hope that kept them picking beans for other farmers; kept them from finally leaving as they talked of doing; kept them knee-deep in other people's dirt; kept them excited about other people's wars; kept them solicitous of white people's children; kept them convinced that some magic "government" was going to lift them up, out and away from that dirt, those beans, those wars.[31]

Reminiscent of the protest marches and riots of the late 1960s, the 1941 march consisted of participants—the old and the young, the lame and the hearty, the women and the children—who were "aggressive and abandoned"; they "smashed the bricks," "split the sacks of limestone," "tore the wire mesh, tipped over wheelbarrows and rolled forepoles down the bank"; they had a "need to kill it all." Also reminiscent of the 1960s, "A lot of them died there" so that others could progress.[32]

It is significant that this event occurs right after the death of Sula, for it points up another example of the dialectical relationship between Sula and the community. Not only does Sula cause the people of the Bottom to unify, albeit temporarily, but also she injects them with a dose of defiance, resistance, and aggressiveness. At first, they equated living with surviving. According to their philosophy, "The purpose of evil was to survive it and they determined (without ever knowing they had made up their minds to do it) to survive white people, tuberculosis, famine and ignorance."[33] Sula's rebelliousness teaches them to confront, then reject, their passive attitude and replace it with a revolutionary consciousness. That is, she "heats up" the Bottom, a heating up process symbolized by the uncharacteristic warm temperature on that day. Thus, in contrast to Barbara Christian's belief that "they do not take from Sula what she has to offer them; the leap into the living, . . . the urge to experiment and thus move forward,"[34] the community people's participation in National Suicide Day (1941) reflects their "leap into the living"— thanks to Sula. Although she limits her analysis to Nel instead of applying it to the entire Bottom community, Karen Stein's comment is more apropos than Christian's: "Nel is symbolically reborn as the surviving self, continuing the process of growth and self-awareness that Sula began."[35] Additionally, as Nel represents the traditional thinking of the community, her recognition of the worth of Sula symbolizes the community's increased consciousness. The community is indeed reborn.[36]

Despite Morrison's effort to disguise the dates, the parallels between the Civil Rights Struggle of the 1960s and the struggle of the Bottom community in 1941, some of which have been noted, are striking. Indeed, it is significant that the chapter following "1941"—"1965"—begins, "Things were so much better in 1965. Or so it seemed."[37] Just as Africans who participated in the Struggle thought that their efforts would defuse the racism raging rampart in the United States, so those of the Bottom, symbolized by Nel, felt that their efforts brought significant changes. Thus the words "or so it seemed" accurately reflect the hopes of both the real and the fictionalized groups. Another echo of the historic struggle of the sixties is Nel's impression of the youth who in 1965 remind her of the aggressive deweys. As the chorus for the Bottom, she also comments on the "fruits" of the struggle. The struggle has enabled a few Africans to progress, that is, to be as much like their oppressors as they can, while the masses of African people continue to struggle for survival: "Everybody [every African] who had made money during the war moved as close as they could to the valley."[38]

This comment on the petty bourgeois element of the African population is one of the few in which Morrison alludes to the role of class in the oppression of African people. The events surrounding the origin of the Bottom represent another such allusion. In *Sula*, the concern of class, whether of the capitalists or the masses, ranks third after sex and race. The few references that are present are made in connection with Helene Wright. However, like the sections on capitalism in *The Bluest Eye*, the passages in reference to Helene's class interests are relatively insignificant in comparison to those on sex and race. Yet they at least show that Morrison was aware of the role class interests play in the lives of African people.

In emphasizing to the community that her name is Helene rather than Helen, in severing her roots with her family, in stifling the imagination of her daughter, in making Nel pull her broad African nose in an effort to make it aquiline, in joining the most conservative church in Medallion, and, most important, in disassociating herself from the African masses (represented by the soldiers) and aligning herself with the white racist train conductor, Helene Wright exposes her class interests. They are the same as those of her oppressors: wealth and status. Helene Wright's disassociation from her people, the clearest example of which occurs during her train trip to New Orleans, is the most significant of these acts. Calling her "gal" and telling her to "get your butt on in there," the white train conductor divulges his belief in Helene's inferiority. For him, "a nigger is a nigger" despite her speech and dress habits, despite her class association. Still, "for no earthly reason" and "like a pup that wags its

tail at the very doorjamb . . . he has been kicked away from,"
Helene Wright "smiled dazzingly and coquettishly" at the conductor while ignoring the two African soldiers who witnessed
the incident.[39]
  The only interaction she has with the masses on an equal basis
is one that is inescapable; she is forced to ask an African woman
the whereabouts of the toilet: "So intense was her distress she
finally brought herself to speak about her problem to a black
woman with four children who got on in Tuscaloosa."[40] Unfortunately, it is not until Helene's need to relieve herself in a
hostile, segregated environment is so acute that she relates to
another African. Living in a racist society, Morrison informs the
reader, Africans—regardless of their wealth and status and regardless of their wish to escape their identity—are seen as one
people:

> All of them, the fat woman and her four children, three boys and a
> girl, Helene and her daughter, squatted there in the four o'clock
> Meridian sun. They did it again in Ellisville, again in Hattiesburg,
> and by the time they reached Slidell, not too far from Lake
> Pontchartrain, Helene could not only fold leaves as well as the fat
> woman, she never felt a stir as she passed the muddy eyes of the men
> who stood like wrecked Dorics under the station roofs of those
> towns.[41]

  The role of class interests will become more pronounced in
Song of Solomon and even more in *Tar Baby* as Morrison's consciousness about the nature of the African's plight in the United
States increases. With the writing of her second novel, however,
the issue of class is only incidental, playing third fiddle to sex
and race.
  That individualism, especially that of the African woman, is
Morrison's emphasis in *Sula* is clarified and substantiated considerably when one analyzes the structural framework of the
story. Despite its periodic inclusion of racial concerns and its
incidental incorporation of class-related issues, the novel begins
and ends with an exposition on individual rather than group
fulfillment. The unrecognized worth of Sula is the message conveyed both by the quote from *The Rose Tattoo* and by Nel's final
words: "O Lord, Sula, . . . girl, girl, girlgirlgirl."[42] Although at

times Morrison seems to doubt her own solution to the African female's exploitation,[43] she ultimately avows that the African woman can obtain freedom from oppression by having an art form:

> Had she paints, or clays, or knew the discipline of dance or strings; had she anything to engage her tremendous curiosity and her gift for metaphor, she might have exchanged the restlessness and preoccupation with whim for an activity that provided her with all she yearned for. And like any artist with no art form, she became dangerous.[44]

Unfortunately, this solution does not take into account the roles of race oppression and class exploitation. It is an idealistic solution that reflects Morrison's own idealism, her own immature analysis of the role of capitalism. She herself will realize the one-sidedness of her proposal; she herself will realize that individual fulfillment is dialectically related to group fulfillment. The former is conditioned by the latter:

> The individual's free will, freedom of action and thought and the full enjoyment of his/her personality should be led by a social consciousness which takes into consideration other people and society in absolute respect of common values, interests and duty.[45]

In contrast to *Sula*, *Song of Solomon* explicitly reveals the suicidal nature of the individual who cuts himself off from his roots, that is, from family, community, and heritage. In effect, Nel and Sula will come together as one balanced individual in the character of Milkman.

Structurally, in its straightforward, largely uncomplicated narrative form, *Sula* is a development of *The Bluest Eye*. Unlike the first novel, *Sula* is not complicated by three narrators. Like the individualist who does not depend on or consider others around her, but leads a life in complete disregard of the other, primarily one narrator relates the story of Sula. The story begins in the present tense, relating the history of Medallion. This present of the novel is the preface or introduction, the untitled first four pages. The events of the rest of the novel, beginning with the chapter entitled "1919," occur in the past. Additionally, the reader is unhampered by passage chapter titles that must be deciphered like codes, and then applied to the chapter contents. Instead, Morrison uses time to organize her narrative. Dates appear as chapter titles that clearly and concisely advance the plot. And unlike the first novel, *Sula* provides us with sufficient and necessary transitions so as to help ideas flow together smoothly and clearly. A case in point is the transition connecting a description of Sula's and Nel's first meeting with one of their visits to Edna Finch's ice cream parlor. The transition device used is the repetition of the word *dreams:*

> Somewhere beneath all that neatness, lay the thing that clothed their dreams. Which was only fitting, for it was in dreams that the two girls had met.[46]

Such a skillful use of transitions is largely absent in *The Bluest Eye.* As a result, the reader must perform the task of mentally providing necessary transitions for the author.

Another skillful method of bringing coherence to her text is Morrison's name or word dropping: Often, she will simply mention a name or word that will later have significance for the reader. For instance, by mentioning the word *smoke*, the reader is informed of Hannah's burning forty pages and two chapters before the actual event. As Barbara Lounsberry insightfully notes, this "narrative technique of gradual disclosure forces the reader into the habit of 'new seeing.' "[47] Clues, forebodings, superstitions, and repetition are all used as transitions. Robins' shitting on the Bottom community, for example, portend Sula's future relationship with it.

All in all, Morrison's structural manipulation of her text will develop as her thematic investigation of the dominant cause of the African's oppression advances; there exists a symbiosis between the two. Structurally, she will become more adept at extirpating unnecessary information that tends to impede the smooth presentation of ideas. Such a weeding-out process is noticeable in *Sula,* for this work omits much of the impotent verbiage of *The Bluest Eye.* The Chicken Little episode seems the only section of *Sula* that does not clearly advance the novel's theme.[48] Thematically, her developing consciousness allows her to perceive the selfish, exploitive nature of individualism under capitalism. Thus, she will never again give her stamp of approval, however tentative, to a character like Sula who has a natural desire for freedom, but who sees it unnaturally as a freedom divorced from the freedom of her people.

4
Song of Solomon
The Struggle for Race and Class Consciousness

Toni Morrison's literary canon is a testimony to the principles of dialectics: it develops; it is interconnected; it reveals contradictions; and it reflects quantity and quality. Her canon also substantiates the premise that literature is a reflection of the society in which it is produced. *The Bluest Eye*, her first novel, explores the question of what it means to be an African in a racist, capitalist society, in this case, the United States. Specifically, Morrison's interest is in exposing the vicious, genocidal effects of racism on the African child. The major shortcoming of the novel, if measured in light of her developing class consciousness, is the solution proposed for eradicating these effects: racial approbation. Despite its weakness, the question posed by *The Bluest Eye*, "Why am I considered inferior?" and the answer, "Because I am an African born in a racist society," are natural starting points for any concerned African struggling for a solution to her people's plight.

In many ways, *Sula* picks up where *The Bluest Eye* ends. *Sula* reflects the evolutionary process that is the trademark of Morrison's canon: the three whores—the Maginot-Line, China, and Poland reappear as Eva, Hannah, and Sula; Pauline Breedlove is Mrs. Helene Wright; Pecola becomes Shadrack; and Claudia is Sula. Of particular interest is Morrison's change in thematic emphasis from her first novel to her second; *Sula* searches for self-identity, not group identity, a change that mirrors the developmental stages of the consciousness of the African masses. Once the African knows who she is, often her struggle becomes one for individual rights. Unfortunately, this struggle for self-development leads some Africans to see themselves in isolation from their people, from the community that has in fact shaped, protected, nurtured, and guided them. This selfish quest for individual fulfillment is certainly that of Sula. Not responsible individualism, hers is a "socially disintegrative version of individualism, that possessive individualism or sanctified rapacity which is extolled by capitalist societies."[1]

By the time she writes *Song of Solomon*, Morrison seems fully conscious of the relationship between the individual African and his community.[2] Evidently, after writing and considering the dilemmas presented and the solutions posed in *The Bluest Eye* and *Sula*, after witnessing and participating in the historic, valiant struggle waged by Africans in the sixties and early seventies, and after being in contact with and editing the works of conscious, revolutionary Africans such as Chinweizu, Morrison has become more aware of the dialectical relationship between capitalism, racism, and sexism.[3] In *Song of Solomon*, she subordinates sexism to both racism and capitalism, realizing that the exploitation of the African woman by the African man is the result of his national and class oppression. That is, sexism is correctly viewed as the consequence of the African's lack of race and class consciousness. Morrison's awareness of these relationships empowers her to create a protagonist whose survival depends on his development of a people consciousness, which, once gained, permanently alters his view of women. One has only to contrast Milkman's relationship with Hagar and Sweet to appreciate the veracity of this statement. After *Song of Solomon*, Morrison will never again create a male protagonist whose race and class consciousness is so underdeveloped that he exploits and oppresses African women.

In fact, this work marks a qualitative leap in Morrison's consciousness as an African and as a writer (for her, the two are inextricably related) in several other regards: she is more aware of the importance of dialectical and historical materialism; she is more aware of the role capitalism plays in the African's exploitation and oppression; she is more aware of the need to create a protagonist who develops during the course of the novel; and she is more aware of the importance of creating a text that allows theme to dictate structure.[4]

To fully appreciate the qualitative leap that Morrison makes in regard to the nature of the African's oppression in the United

States and in regard to her artistic dexterity, her protagonist's growth should be viewed as three distinct yet interconnected developmental stages that lead to his increased race and class consciousness: the preliminal stage, the liminal stage, and the postliminal stage.[5] There are general characteristics peculiar to each as well as particular characteristics associated with the protagonist's heightened consciousness.

In the opening chapters of the novel, Milkman's low level of consciousness in regard to his people's race and class oppression manifests itself in his nickname. Ironically, Macon Dead III acquires it as a result of his extended nursing period, for instead of helping him to become more attuned to his mother and her needs, this lengthy bonding period proves ineffectual in a society that promotes selfish individualism above love and concern for humankind: Milkman is emotionally estranged from Ruth Dead as he is from all women with whom he interacts. As his nickname suggests, he milks women, pilfering their love and giving nothing in return. Even at age thirty-one, he knows very little about women, an ignorance made evident by his inability to distinguish his sisters from his mother.[6] Nor can he conceive of women as human beings, not even his mother: "Never had he thought of his mother as a person, a separate individual, with a life apart from allowing or interfering with his own."[7] Women, in general, have value only as "need providers" for Milkman. Therefore, his act of urinating on Lena becomes an act symbolic of his pissing on all women, Hagar in particular.

It is Hagar who is most exploited. While she genuinely loves Milkman, he loves her solely as a receptacle in which to empty his lust, seldom taking her anywhere except the movies and considering her his "private honey pot."[8] Eventually, even sex with her becomes a bore, being "so free, so abundant." So, as a pimp taking leave of his whore, Milkman pays Hagar for twelve years of service and writes her a thank you letter, reminding her that they are first cousins and self-righteously telling himself that he is performing a selfless act. Like Sula, Milkman—in this liminal stage—shits on those around him, particularly the women of the novel.[9]

Pilate is no exception. From her, as from Hagar, he receives a love both free and abundant. Wallowing in it, Milkman feels for "the first time in his life that he remembered being completely happy."[10] Most important, it is because of Pilate—the pilot—that he is steered in a conscious direction. Through her acknowledgement of, dignity in, and proudness of her Africanness, despite her lack of material wealth, Milkman gets his first lesson in race and class consciousness: "While she looked as poor as everyone said she was, something was missing from her eyes that should have confirmed it."[11] Like Pilate, Milkman must learn to respect his African self and to realize that money does not ensure happiness. Instead of killing the potential savior of his people as does her biblical namesake, Dead Pilate breathes life into Milkman.[12] It is she who first forces him to confront his identity as the living dead who sucks the life force from his people; from her he learns the essence of life. Devouring the fruity, yolky core of life and speaking in a voice that reminded Milkman of little round pebbles that bumped against each other, Pilate is nature personified. She is, in fact, earth mother. What Milkman gives her in return for life is the murder of her daughter and the theft of her father. Significantly, it is not until the Shalimar Hunt, when he learns the importance of whispering to the trees and the ground, touching them, "as a blind man caresses a page of Braille, pulling meaning through his fingers," that Milkman appreciates the life that this earth mother provides him.[13]

It is quite apropos, in light of his surname, that Milkman at first reciprocates Pilate's love with death. Like all the members of the Macon Dead household, he is dead. Even the family car, a spotlessly clean Packard, is regarded by the community as a hearse, a car that cauterizes the ties between the living (the community) and the dead (the Dead family). As the community voice of the novel, the Greek chorus, Freddie's evaluation of the Dead is valid: "A dead man ain't no man. A dead man is a corpse."[14] At this point in his life, Milkman Dead is neither a man (exploiting all women with whom he comes into contact), nor a human being in general. He is both psychologically and emotionally dead.

Additional manifestations of Milkman's low level of consciousness are his overall state of confusion and his association with things behind him. His disconcertedness is best exemplified by his obsession with flying. Yet while he seems bombarded with images of flight and imbued with a natural sense of flying, he experiences feelings of flying blindly. And, of course, he is. Not knowing his past, he is unsure of the future: "Infinite possibilities and enormous responsibilities stretched out before him, but he was not prepared to take advantage of the former, or accept the burden of the latter."[15] Unconscious of the fact that responsibilities are an integral part of life, Milkman lives the limbo life of the living dead, always struggling "to make up his mind whether to go forward or to turn back."[16] His face reveals the confusion he feels, for "it was all very tentative," and "it lacked a coherence, a coming together of the features into a total self."[17] This confusion will last until Milkman immerses himself in the life of his people; it is a confusion symbolized by a short limb because, as the narrator makes clear, this short limb is more the creation of his own mind than an actual fact:

> By the time Milkman was fourteen he had noticed that one of his legs was shorter than the other. When he stood barefoot and straight as a pole, his left foot was about half an inch off the floor. So he never stood straight; he slouched or leaned or stood with a hip thrown out, and he never told anybody about it—ever. . . . The deformity was mostly in his mind.[18]

In spite of Milkman's lack of consciousness, he seems instinctively aware of the importance of the past, for he is obsessed with things behind him. In fact, "it was becoming a habit—this concentration on things behind him."[19] Moreover, he is aware that everyone moves in the opposite direction as he, "going the direction he was coming from,"[20] a suggestion that they already have knowledge of their past, which directs them to their future. However, he is not yet prepared to turn his instinctual awareness into a conscious search for his history.

Not only do the general characteristics associated with Milkman help the critic to assess the protagonist's level of consciousness in the opening chapters of the novel, but also particular characteristics in regard to his race and class consciousness prove invaluable clues. In regard to race, the extent of Milkman's consciousness can be gauged by several factors—his relationship with the local community as well as his awareness of national events that affect African people. So isolated is he from his people that he is the last to know about the relationship between Henry Porter and his sister, First Corinthians; he is the last to know about the Seven Days; and he is the last to know about Emmett Till's murder. Once he is aware of these occurrences, he at first shows little concern for all except that which affects him directly, the courtship between Henry Porter and First Corinthians. Milkman is bored by all other events, revealing his complete estrangement from the community. When informed of the vicious murder of the fourteen-year-old Till, a murder which elicited the sympathy of both Europeans and Africans worldwide, Milkman replies: "Yeah, well, fuck Till. I'm the one in trouble."[21] Such statements as this reflect Milkman's need to develop the race consciousness, which will allow him to see himself and other African people as one, having a common identity, a common history, and a common struggle.

The protagonist's class consciousness is just as weak as his race awareness. Believing in his father's capitalist philosophy that to own things is the essence of life, Milkman has little regard for the masses in the community, and, consequently, they have little regard for him.[22] Being one of those masses, Feather throws Milkman out of his pool hall, rightfully associating the young Macon with his father. If Milkman is to establish close ties with the community, he must rid himself of dead weight—that Macon Dead mentality. He must begin to love his people more than his money, which will require that he, like Pilate, commit class suicide: "She gave up, apparently, all interest in table manners or hygiene, but acquired a deep concern for and about human relationships."[23] As for now, Milkman's interest in life is "wherever the party is," and his associations, with the exception of Guitar, are with the petty bourgeois St. Honore crowd.[24]

It is not until Milkman begins to question the people and events around him that his consciousness begins to develop, that he enters the liminal stage of discovery and growth. Although this period of liminality actually begins in chapter 3—"Now he questioned them. Questioned everybody"[25]—it is not sufficiently developed until chapter 5 when he has discovered the answers to crucial questions of identity.

Chapter 5 begins with Milkman's death wish, an attempt by him to renounce all that he has learned thus far because such knowledge brings with it an acceptance of the responsibility of adulthood in general and Africanhood in particular:

Above all he wanted to escape what he knew, escape the implications of what he had been told. And all he knew in the world about the world was what other people had told him. He felt like a garbage pail for the actions and hatreds of other people. He himself did nothing. Except for the one time he had hit his father, he had never acted independently, and that act, his only one, had brought unwanted knowledge, too, as well as some responsibility for that knowledge.[26]

In his determination to renounce all, Milkman patiently, resignedly awaits the revengeful, deadly rage of Hagar, laying in "Guitar's bed face-up in the sunlight, trying to imagine how it would feel when the ice pick entered his neck."[27] Pregnant with images of death—words such as *indifference, silence, fatigue,* and *lazy righteousness* are used throughout—this chapter reflects Milkman's readiness to "roll over and die," his readiness to become an egg, easily cracked and easily eaten, because "afterward there would be no remembrance of who he was or where."[28]

Milkman's death wish is a necessary phase in his development, for his confrontation with and subsequent defiance of death teach him both sensitivity and sympathy, allowing him to look beyond self. In actuality, this attempted physical suicide prefaces and prefigures his class suicide. It is in this liminal state, a period of growth though not a full state of consciousness, that, for the first time, Milkman "rubbed the ankle of this short leg," feeling a sensation that is dialectically related to his increased consciousness.[29] To the extent that his race and class consciousness develop, so does his leg develop, for Milkman's belief in his short limb was "mostly in his mind." It is in this liminal state that he feels "a quick beat of something like remorse" when he remembers Guitar's story about a doe, that one should never kill a female deer."[30] Such physical and emotional occurrences are clearly indicative of Milkman's maturing consciousness.

Extending from chapters 3 to 9, from his attempted suicide to his recognition of his wish to live, a wish that brings with it responsibility, Milkman's liminal stage of development can be documented in particular by his increasing race and class awareness. With his newly gained sensitivity, Milkman asks Guitar questions about his best friend's strange behavior: "We've been friends a long time Guitar. There's nothing you don't know about me. I can tell you anything—whatever our differences, I know I can trust you. But for some time now it's been a one-way street."[31] Of course, Milkman, blinded to all people and all things except himself, created the one-way street. In point of fact, this occasion marks the first in which he has asked his friend questions that have not concerned the Dead family. Not just questioning his friend's lifestyle, Milkman argues with Guitar about the morality of the Seven Days' philosophy, saying, "But people who lynch and slice off people's balls—they're crazy, Guitar, crazy,"[32] and asking, "What about the nice ones? Some whites made sacrifices for Negroes. Real sacrifices."[33] When juxtaposed with "Fuck Till," these concerns in regard to racial issues reflect a different, more sensitive Milkman. They do not, however, reflect a fully conscious protagonist. For Milkman is only questioning the philosophy of people who "sound like that red-headed Negro named X,"[34] not proposing an alternative solution for eradicating the oppression of African people.

Milkman's awareness of race is made more poignant by his personal confrontation with the police. Stripped of his dignity, emasculated like millions of other African men throughout the world, Milkman is overwhelmed with shame:

> Shame at being spread-eagled, fingered, and handcuffed. . . . But nothing was like the shame he felt as he watched and listened to Pilate. Not just her Aunt Jemima act, but the fact that she was both adept at it and willing to do it—for him.[35]

This incident helps Milkman to distinguish between those Africans who assume the role of the Uncle Tom or the Aunt Jemima as a way of life and those who do so as a way of survival. While he feels proud of Pilate, who sacrifices her dignity to free him from jail even when he was prepared "to knock her down if she had come into the room while he was in the act of stealing" from her, he feels ashamed of his father, who "buckle[s] before the policemen."[36] And the fact that he sees more dignity and life in the poor Pilate than in the rich Macon increases his class consciousness. That is, the incident crystallizes for him the way in which capitalism, with its emphasis on money and status, affects African people who ascribe to its values: they will always be petty capitalists, puppets "with an accomodating 'we all understand how it is' smile."[37]

This incident with the police is the second that contributes to

Milkman's developing class consciousness. The first results from
the appearance of a white peacock, symbolizing both the race
and the wealth of the ruling class in the United States. Ironically,
this peacock appears while Guitar and Milkman are planning to
rob Pilate's "gold." Significantly, it is Milkman who first sees it,
"poised on the roof of a long low building that served as head-
quarters for Nelson Buick."[38] Equating both flight and money
with freedom, Milkman asks Guitar why a peacock can't fly. His
friend replies, "Wanna fly, you got to give up the shit that weighs
you down."[39] Although Milkman is not yet fully conscious of the
connection between the diamondlike tail of the peacock and the
"gold" he is planning to steal from Pilate, Dead weight that will
only impede his search for identity, this incident does contribute
to his growing class consciousness.

Milkman's postliminal stage, which marks the height of his
consciousness, is characterized by his initiation into a new society, the society of the Shalimar hunters. Like the preliminal
and liminal stages, this stage is symbolized by linguistic, psychological, and physical changes. As his race and class consciousness develop so does his language. Irresponsible,
individualistic statements such as "Yeah, well, fuck Till," which
characterize his preliminality and which symbolize his complete
insensitivity to the plight of African people, are replaced by the
Africanized voice of collective communion, a communion
shared by all living matter.[40] Psychologically, Milkman accepts
the responsibility of adulthood and Africanhood: "He had
stopped evading things, sliding through, over, and around diffi-
culties."[41] Having learned to respect the natural world more than
the material one and having gained the ability to laugh at himself, Milkman has become a psychologically balanced individual:

> There was nothing here [on the Shalimar hunt] to help him—not his
> money, his car, his father's reputation, his suit, or his shoes. In fact
> they hampered him. . . .[42] They [the Shalimar hunters] hooted and
> laughed all the way back to the car, teasing Milkman, egging him on
> to tell more about how scared he was. And he told them. Laughing
> too, hard, loud, and long. Really laughing.[43]

After "the pain in his short leg [becomes] so great he began to
limp and hobble," physically, Milkman becomes balanced as
well: he no longer limps; both legs are equal.[44]

In regard to race, his high level of consciousness is exemplified on two occasions, when he learns of his grandfather's murder and when he participates in the Shalimar hunt. Milkman first learns of his grandfather's murder from Pilate, but he hears these details during a time when his race consciousness is at its lowest level. When he hears of the murder a second time, from Reverend Cooper, he asks, infuriated, why the Danville Africans did not seek revenge: " 'And nobody did anything?' Milkman wondered at his own anger. He hadn't felt angry when he first heard about it. Why now?"[45] His anger is aroused on this occasion because of his heightened awareness of himself in connection with other African people. Eventually, this consciousness manifests itself in a sincere love for and understanding of his people, even for the slightly unbalanced Day, who comes to kill him:

> But something had maimed him, scarred him like Reverend Cooper's knot, like Saul's missing teeth, and like his own father. He felt a sudden rush of affection for them all, and out there under the sweet gum tree, within the sound of men tracking a bobcat, he thought he understood Guitar now. Really understood him.[46]

During the hunt, Milkman's class consciousness sharpens as well. Learning the insignificance of money and status when juxtaposed with a true communion with African people, Milkman commits class suicide.[47] While it is true that the seeds of his decision to bond with the African masses instead of those having his wealth and status are planted when he first meets Pilate, his conscious decision to do so germinates from his Shalimar experiences. According to anthropologist Arnold van Gennep, one must undergo several initiation rites prior to being incorporated into a new society. In Milkman's case, these rites are related to his increased class consciousness.

First, the initiate must be stripped of all that is psychologically and physically associated with his old society. This initiation rite entails a physical descent into a cave, an enclosing or engulfing that usually signals a baptism and an imminent rebirth. Milkman experiences both. Entering Hunters Cave with all the material, artificial trappings of capitalist society—a wad of money, an expensive watch, a beige three-piece suit, a "button-down light-blue shirt and black string tie," a snap-brim hat, a suitcase with a bottle of scotch, and beautiful Florsheim shoes—Milkman emerges an offspring of nature, with water-ruined suit, soggy shoes, and a broken watch.

Second, the initiate must be cognizant of the mores of the new society. In Milkman's case, he must learn that he cannot exploit the people. He can neither show nor receive gratitude with money. Because humanism is a traditional African principle valued more than money and held in esteem more by the African masses than the African petty bourgeois, Circe, Fred Garnet, and the Shalimar community are offended by Milkman's capitalist behavior:

> They looked at his skin and saw it was as black as theirs, but they knew he had the heart of the white men who came to pick them up in the trucks when they needed anonymous, faceless laborers.[48]

Just as important as the principle of humanism, Milkman must learn egalitarianism, the inherent equality of every human being. Prior to the hunt, he thinks himself so superior to the Shalimar people that he sees them not as unique individuals, but as one large anonymous group. For instance, with the Shalimar men in hearing distance, he condescendingly asks the storeowner (whom he only assumes to be Mr. Solomon because he never asks the storeowner his name) if one of the men can help him: "He looked at the men sitting around the store. 'You think maybe one of them could help with the car?' he asked Mr. Solomon."[49]

Third, he must put his newly learned humanistic theories into practice by participating in the rituals of the new society. Milkman does so by agreeing to go on the hunt, a ritual that proves to be a psychological and physical test of strength, allowing him to shed his old capitalist-oriented ideology and replace it with a new people-oriented, nature-oriented ideology. In the true spirit of baptism and rebirth, Milkman rethinks his past behavior and contemplates the new life awaiting him, a life that will allow him, like the men of Shalimar, to commune with all of nature's children:

> It was more than tracks Calvin was looking for—he whispered to the trees, whispered to the ground, touched them, as a blind man caresses a page of Braille, pulling meaning through his fingers.[50]

His new, revolutionized consciousness enables him to confront and to regret his old way of life: "The consequences of Milkman's own stupidity would remain, and regret would always outweigh the things he was proud of having done."[51]

Significantly, it is not until after Milkman has revolutionized his consciousness in regard to race oppression and class exploitation that he sheds his sexist views of women. Prior to this increased awareness, Milkman, as his name suggests, milks the life out of women, giving them nothing in return. As pointed out, so reactionary is his view of women that he has difficulty distinguishing his mother from his sisters and rarely thinks of any of them. Pissing on Lena, squealing on First Corinthians, spying on Ruth, stealing from Pilate, and murdering Hagar—all are evidence of Milkman's low level of consciousness. At the time he commits these acts, he is not aware of that oneness which connects African people, that pissing on Lena is like pissing on himself, that the sexual exploitation and murder of Hagar are the sexual exploitation and murder of himself. As the prophetic Pilate explains to Hagar, all are acts of self-hatred: "How can he not love your hair? It's the same hair that grows out of his own armpits. The same hair that crawls up out of his crotch on up his stomach."[52]

Not only actions, but also words are early reflections of Milkman's lack of consciousness in regard to women. He tells Hagar, "If you keep your hands just that way and then bring them down straight, straight and fast, you can drive that knife right smack in your cunt." Such backwards, genocidal acts committed and words voiced against the mothers of his race can only find life in a society that promotes profit above human welfare, the individual above the group. It is this priceless treasure of knowledge that Milkman gains by the end of the novel.

Quite noticeably, his consciousness in regard to women begins to rise when he discovers some of his mother's past and heightens even more after his participation in the hunt. Earlier, Guitar had warned Milkman against exploiting women by relating an incident in which Guitar killed a doe; "A man shouldn't do that."[53] This warning, however, goes unheeded until Milkman takes an active interest in his mother's well-being: "He remembered Guitar's story about killing one. . . . 'A man shouldn't do that.' Milkman felt a quick beat of something like remorse."[54] But like the prickly feeling he gets in his knee, this fleeting sense of sympathy reflects only the beginnings of growth and healing, not the completion of them. Significantly, "He shook it [the feeling of remorse] off and resumed" his old way of thinking, talking, and acting. That is, he proceeds to kill the doe. In this case, when he discovers Ruth at her father's grave site, he kills her with words: "You come to lay down on your father's grave? Is that what you've been doing all these years? Spending a night every now and then with your father?"[55]

It is not until Milkman has stripped himself of the ruling class's views of race (intraracial, in this case) and class superiority that he is able to see women as his equals. This rite of passage is not complete until the Shalimar hunt, during which Milkman first becomes conscious, then ashamed of his exploitation of Hagar, "whom he'd thrown away like a wad of chewing gum after the flavor was gone—she had a right to try to kill him too."[56] It is only after this event that he fully understands the reciprocal nature of human relationships:

> She [Sweet] put salve on his face. He washed her hair. She sprinkled talcum on his feet. He straddled her behind and massaged her back. She put witch hazel on his swollen neck. He made up the bed. She gave him gumbo to eat. He washed the dishes. She washed his clothes and hung them out to dry. He scoured her tub. She ironed his shirt and pants. He gave her fifty dollars. She kissed his mouth. He touched her face. She said please come back. He said I'll see you tonight.[57]

Perhaps the most significant evidence of Milkman's awareness of the principle of reciprocity as related to women is his commitment to guide Pilate to Shalimar to bury her father's bones, just as she had guided him to bury the Dead in him. In fact, with his revolutionized consciousness—which prizes humanism and egalitarianism—he becomes the pilot, the source of life. Thus, the name "Milkman" is transformed to signify that which is positive, not negative. The protagonist becomes the milkman who is capable of carrying the source of life for those in need. The emphasis here is on the word *capable*, for while Milkman's race and class consciousness develop sufficiently to allow him to recreate self, it never reaches the point where Milkman moves beyond self-healing to "other-healing."

Still, Morrison's creation of a character who must develop both race and class awareness prior to developing an egalitarian and humanistic view of women reflects her own increased consciousness of the dialectical relationship between the African male's nation-class oppression and his exploitation of African women. Such a qualitative leap in her ability to analyze the nature of capitalism empowers her to structure a text that is qualitatively better than the first two. Evidently, Morrison's understanding that an awareness of the particular nature of the African's oppression must precede the development of a viable solution increases her awareness of the dialectical relationship between meaning and structure. The first must dictate the latter. Such a mature understanding of the role of narrative structure is reflected in *Song of Solomon*. The overall text, the chapters, and the sentences within the chapters reflect this symbiotic relationship between form and content.

First, Morrison uses flight as structure for the overall text. *Song of Solomon* begins and ends with unsuccessful flight attempts: Robert Smith's begins the novel; Milkman's ends the novel. Richard K. Barksdale comments on the use of flight as structure when he writes,

> The story that is related about [the characters'] experiences does not have a definable beginning, middle and end. The novel begins with a black man attempting to fly and ends with a black man attempting to fly. In other words, the pattern of narration is circular, not linear.[58]

That the structure is circular suggests the absence of a solution, the failure of the protagonist (and his precursor) to share the liberating knowledge he has gained in order to create an environment free of oppression. That is, the unsuccessful nature of both flights reflects both men's lack of responsibility to the African community. Through their own admission or commission, they reveal their guilt: Smith leaves a suicidal note asking forgiveness; Milkman flies away despite his new awareness that true flight for humanity in general and the African in particular is the ability to fly without ever leaving the ground.[59] Moreover, the facts that Smith's death and Milkman's birth occur almost simultaneously enhance the structural relationship between the two characters and the concept of flight.

Second, Morrison divides her chapters into two parts: the first primarily chronicles Milkman's lack of consciousness in regard to race and class; the second predominantly concentrates on his developing consciousness in regard to them.

Third, the author uses parallel sentences to reflect equal relationships or equal actions. Such is the case when the newly awakened Milkman participates in a ritual of reciprocity with Sweet.[60] Balanced sentence parts are used as well to inform the reader of close relationships between characters. Referring to Pilate and Ruth, Morrison writes: "The singer, standing at the back of the crowd, was as poorly dressed as the doctor's daughter was well dressed."[61]

Morrison's practice of briefly describing relationships, events, and people she is not yet prepared to discuss adds to the quality of this novel; it is a skillful method of creating a coherent text. At the beginning of the novel, for example, Freddie is referred to as "a gold-toothed man" and Guitar, "the cat-eyed boy." Both names are withheld. This narrative method requires that the reader mentally store the descriptive phases until the characters are formally introduced. In this way, the reader ceases to be a passive bystander, but becomes an active partner in creating textual coherence by sewing together an earlier section of the novel with a later one.

Additionally, Morrison manipulates time much more skillfully in this work than in her first two. Transition sentences such as "That was the beginning. Now it was all going to end" transport the reader from the past to the present without the nauseating jolt of an air pocket. Such sophisticated use of transitions appears between as well as within chapters. As a case in point, the parental role of Guitar and Pilate in relationship to Hagar serves as the transition device that cements chapters 5 and 6. Chapter 5 ends with Pilate's effort to keep Ruth's mind off Hagar's attempt to kill Milkman:

> Pilate would have moved on immediately except for her brother's wife, who was dying of lonelessness then, and seemed to be dying of it now as she sat at the table across from her sister-in-law listening to her life story, which Pilate was making deliberately long to keep Ruth's mind off Hagar.[62]

Chapter 6 begins with Guitar's effort to take Hagar home after one of her failed attempts to murder Milkman: "I [Guitar] took her home. She was standing in the middle of the room when I got there. So I just took her home. Pitiful. Really pitiful."[63]

Perhaps one of the most significant gauges of Morrison's maturation in regard to structure is her ability to match form with content. Chapter 13 is the clearest example of this ability. Coming just after the Shalimar hunt, during and after which Milkman evidences his heightened consciousness in regard to race and class, chapter 13 serves as structural proof of Morrison's theme: "You can never go off and leave a body." Thematically, it picks up in the middle of chapter 5, detailing the events surrounding Hagar's demise after Milkman makes his most cruel, race-killing statement concerning the mutilation of her sexual organs.[64] Milkman's selfish individualism affects all Africans: Hagar's death in general and the destruction of her reproductive capability in particular mean the death of future generations of African people. By placing chapter 13 between ones which evidence Milkman's development, Morrison reminds the reader that the past must serve as a useful guide to the future. Thus, even though Milkman does not understand the full significance of Sweet's question—"Who did he [Solomon] leave behind"—the reader does. Neither Solomon nor Milkman uses knowledge responsibility—to forge a better future for their kind.

In structure and in theme, *Song of Solomon* is a more advanced work of art than either *The Bluest Eye* or *Sula*. Thematically, Morrison understands that the African in the United States experiences national and class oppression. Additionally, she is aware that the African male's exploitation of the African female is related to this oppression; that it is, in fact, the result of it. Such clearsightedness enables her, for the first time, to create a male as protagonist, one who must first become conscious of himself in relationship to his people; then and as a consequence, reject the individualistic, vulturistic class aspirations of his oppressor before experiencing a wholesome relationship with a woman.[65] Structurally, Morrison's consciousness of the importance of discovering the cause of the African's oppression before proposing a solution empowers her to subordinate structure to meaning.

Yet, in spite of the growth evidenced in her writing of *Song of Solomon*, Morrison has not yet sufficiently matured to understand that while the African is exploited both racially and economically, his economic exploitation forms the basis for his national oppression. In the words of Kwame Nkrumah, while "capitalist exploitation and race oppression are complementary, the removal of [the first] ensures the removal of the other."[66] Without such an understanding, she cannot propose a viable solution, the eradication of capitalism. This is the thematic weakness of the novel. By the end of it, Milkman sees himself as an African exploited by capitalism and oppressed by racism, but he offers no solution to this dilemma. Instead, he surrenders to exploitation and oppression. Rather than moving beyond the act of defeatism exhibited by his forefather, he repeats it: Knowing what Shalimar knew, he surrenders to the air.[67]

Thus, it is interesting that Milkman possesses the knowledge, the theory needed to help abolish the exploitation and oppression of African people, needed to revolutionize their consciousness, but he chooses not to use this knowledge as a weapon of change. He fails to make his contribution to humanity.[68] In contrast, Guitar does act, but his is misguided action, for he does not have the knowledge base of Milkman. Both knowledge and action are needed because "practice without thought is blind; thought without practice is empty."[69] Milkman and Guitar must come, that is, fly, together to create the conscious action so desperately needed by African people. And they do, but the conscious, action-oriented offspring they create by such a union does not materialize until *Tar Baby*.[70]

Because they are dialectically related, not only does the theme of *Song of Solomon* indicate the maturation that Toni Morrison must yet develop, but so does the structure. While it is an advancement of the narrative forms of her first two novels, it does not reflect her fullest consciousness of the nature of capitalism. Once she is at her highest peak, Morrison will reject all those structural elements that reflect the injustices of capitalism, in particular the notion that one human being is superior to another. For instance, in *Tar Baby* she will not merely rely on an omniscient narrator, one who knows all despite his lack of involvement. Rather, she will create a structure that allows for narrative contributions from all the major characters. In this manner, she creates a text that is much more socialist in design.

5

Tar Baby

A Reflection of Morrison's Developed Class Consciousness

Class struggle, the struggle between the ruling class and the subject class, is the thematic emphasis of Toni Morrison's fourth work, *Tar Baby*. Racism, the primary focus of *The Bluest Eye*, is discussed as a coequal but consequential cause of the African's oppression. The struggle between the sexes, having been explored in *Sula* and resolved in *Song of Solomon*, gets little of the author's attention, for Morrison has sufficiently matured to understand that the fundamental cause of the African's oppression is the exploitive economic system of capitalism and its overseas extension, imperialism.[1] Thus, racism and sexism, although equally oppressive, are treated as by-products of capitalism. To eradicate the latter ensures the eradication of the former two. In *Tar Baby*, Morrison's increased consciousness is reflected in her ability and commitment to explore this cause-and-effect relationship between class, race, and sex.

Morrison's heightened class awareness creates qualitative changes in both the thematic and structural development of her fourth novel. Thematically, for the first time, the author chooses a setting outside the borders of the United States—Dominique and its surrounding islands. Place, then, in *Tar Baby*, is just as crucial to our understanding of the novel's dilemma and denouement, and to our understanding of the author's own consciousness, as it is in Joseph Conrad's *Heart of Darkness*. Place reveals both Morrison's awareness of the innate viciousness of capitalism and her understanding that "all peoples of African descent, whether they live in North or South America, the Caribbean or any other part of the world are Africans," have a common oppressor, wage a

common struggle, and need a common solution.[2] Then, too, the
choice of the Caribbean as setting allows Morrison and the reader
to get a more objective view of the United States, a view not
dissimilar to that of Gideon: "The U.S. is a bad place to die in."[3]

The second qualitative leap evidenced in Morrison's theme is
her use of European-Americans as major characters. In earlier
works, they serve as minor characters, usually invisible foes who
are hinted at, referred to, laughed about, or ignored altogether. In
Tar Baby their rise to prominence parallels Morrison's rise in
consciousness, for she now understands the dialectical role they
play as the ruling class in the African's oppression, a role that can
be neither ignored nor minimized. Significant, therefore, is the
fact that she does not choose Europeans of the lower or middle
classes, but those of the ruling class. Moreover, these Europeans
have a direct connection to the exploitation of African people in
Dominique and in the United States, revealing Morrison's un-
clouded understanding that the capitalists and imperialists are
one and the same.

The nature of the struggle of African people in the novel is an
additional piece of evidence that reflects the qualitative difference between this work and earlier ones. Unlike Pecola
Breedlove, who struggles with the question of racial approbation,
Sula, who struggles against the traditional role of African
women, and Milkman, who individually struggles with the issues of race and class, the two protagonists in *Tar Baby* must
struggle together to resolve their opposing class interests in order
to unite.[4] Symbolically, they reflect the schism that exists in the
African community, the class conflict that African people must
resolve in order to form an effective, unified force against their
primary enemy, capitalism/imperialism. What Morrison does in
Tar Baby is raise the question all Africans must ask themselves:
Do I identify with my oppressor or my people? In light of this
question, Morrison examines several other crucial ones: First, if
the African rejects the capitalist way of life, what is a viable
alternative? Second, can African people negate history by returning to a pre-slave-trade, precolonial existence? Third, can there
exist "people's capitalism," "enlightened capitalism," "class
peace," or "class harmony" between two groups of people whose
interests are diametrically opposed?[5] In other words, can Jadine
and Son coexist in harmony? The ending of *Tar Baby* provides

answers to all three questions. It reveals Morrison's own clarity in regard to the irreconcilability of the interests of the ruling and subject classes. And while she clearly rejects vulturistic capitalism, she just as clearly rejects the naive prescription of Kenneth Kaunda, President of Zambia, for an African communal socialism, a way of life that seeks to return to a glorified past without the benefit of modern technology, modern science, or modern consciousness. Unfortunately, however, she does not provide a viable alternative existence for African people. This is the thematic weakness of the novel.

Structurally, too, *Tar Baby* reflects Toni Morrison's heightened consciousness. She produces a work that reflects the positive principles of traditional African society: humanism, collectivism, and egalitarianism.[6] Each of her major characters—Son, Jadine, Sydney, Ondine, Valerian, Margaret, and Therese—has an opportunity to present his or her particular views on self and others. And while there is an omniscient narrator, this narrator is not given a role superior to that of each of the others but unobstrusively highlights rather than prescribes or defines significant character thoughts and actions. Such a narrative technique offers a more balanced, more objective picture from which to judge the characters.

As class struggle is the dominant theme in *Tar Baby*, it is useful to analyze the novel first by employing a structural framework that examines the two major forces in contention: the ruling class and the subject class (sometimes referred to as the "people class"). It is also useful to analyze Morrison's attempt to reconcile these forces in bringing together Jadine and Son.

Valerian Street, as well as all who share his aspirations, is a symbol of American capitalism and imperialism. Indeed, he is a typical capitalist who has made his fortune by exploiting the labor of the African masses and by stealing their land. And it is quite significant that his wealth emanates from the production of candy, the main ingredients of which—sugar and cocoa—come from the Caribbean, once the sugar capital of the western world.[7] This economic fact is made even more poignant after Valerian fires Gideon and Therese for stealing a couple of apples. From Son's, Morrison's, and the reader's perspective, Valerian "had been able to dismiss with a flutter of the fingers the people whose sugar and cocoa had allowed him to grow old in regal comfort."[8]

Quite aptly, he is named after a plant, the dried roots of which have small clusters of white or pinkish flowers used medicinally as a sedative. And as his name suggests, Valerian is asleep throughout most of his adult life, unconscious of or unconcerned by the exploitive manner in which he has accumulated his wealth, ignorant of the physical and psychological abuse of his child by his own wife, unsympathetic to the feelings of his servants, and most important for Morrison and her audience, insensitive to the plight of African people.[9] Somnolently, with all of the lush, uncultured, living nature around him, he builds a greenhouse in which to incubate himself from life, but primarily, and in true capitalist fashion, in which to control life. In his words, it is "a place of controlled ever-flowering life." So estranged from life is Valerian that he is incapable of love despite the fact that his name suggests this human emotion, for the reader may be tempted to associate Valerian with the name of that day in February on which love is celebrated. Bickering, ridiculing, and name calling constitute the extent of the communication between him and his wife. With his son, Michael, he has no communication. And after thirty years of faithful butlering and cooking, Sydney and Ondine are thought of as mere Uncle Toms.[10] Responding to Valerian's inhumanity, Ondine shouts, "I may be a cook, Mr. Street, but I'm a person too."[11] For Valerian, however, one's worth as a human being is measured only by nonhuman values: wealth and status.

Since his desire is to control life, not live in it, Valerian uses his money to relate to other human beings. He buys Margaret expensive clothes and pays Jadine's college tuition. In fact, it is not until he is confronted with the physical and psychological abuse of his son that he exhibits some genuine emotion, but even this emotional display reeks more of self-pity for his ignorance of the abuse than sorrow for the psychological well-being of his wife and child. For instead of seeking help for Margaret and searching for Michael, Valerian retreats to his greenhouse and to his childhood: "Valerian wanted his own youth again and a place to spend it."[12]

While it is true that the ruling class in the United States (all of whom are of European descent) consists of those who own and control the means of production, it is also true that there are those (including Africans) who so ardently wish to belong to this class that they exhibit the same behavioral patterns, dress in the same manner, use the same language patterns, and, most unfortunately, share the same ideology as those of their oppressors. Often referred to as the petty bourgeois, this group of people exists between two worlds, denied entry into the ruling class due to their lack of wealth and/or their skin color and refusing to identify with the African masses to whom they owe allegiance. Jadine, as well as Sydney and Ondine, symbolizes the African petty bourgeois.

Called Kingfish and Beulah by Margaret Street, Sydney and Ondine symbolize those unconscious servants who identify more with their employers and their employers' culture than they do with their own people and their own culture. Sydney, in the light of day, proudly refers to himself as "one of those industrious Philadelphia Negroes—the proudest people in the race"—ignorant of the fact that in the dark of night his "refreshing" dreams of childhood days in Baltimore are what give him the stamina to cater to Valerian's whims.[13] Ondine, painfully reminiscent of Mrs. Breedlove in *The Bluest Eye*, calls the Streets' kitchen "my kitchen" and does not want it violated by the African masses. Living a secondhand life, they accordingly have secondhand furniture, secondhand visitors ("No visitors ever came" for them) and a secondhand daughter (Because Jadine was a niece, Ondine's relationship with her "was without the stress of a mother-daughter relationship").[14] Perhaps most significant is that they are surnamed Childs, for they are indeed the children of Valerian who do as they are told. Yet, despite the humiliation and degradation of being adults treated as children, they both share the racist, capitalist ideology of their employers. As a consequence, they recognize no bond between themselves and Gideon and Therese, the other African servants who work for the Streets. In fact, Sydney and Ondine are unable to distinguish between them, an unwillingness to recognize "lower class" Africans as human beings with unique identities: Gideon is referred to as Yardman, and Therese is thought to be several different Marys. On the whole and in true capitalist fashion, these Childses respond to the other Africans as if all African people look alike.

Not only do they embrace the same racist stereotypes as do their exploiters, but the Childses use the same negative jargon to refer to people who look just like them! The poor African masses are niggers who steal; in contrast, the Childses are Negroes, respectable Africans.[15] It is a respectability that prevents them from seeing themselves as a part of the African masses. For instance, in seeking to disassociate himself from Son, Sydney proudly reveals his ignorance of African culture:

> I am a Phil-a-delphia Negro mentioned in the book of the very same name. My people owned drugstores and taught school while yours were still cutting their faces open so as to be able to tell one of you from the other.[16]

Indeed, it is only by understanding Sydney's petty bourgeois mentality that we can account for his reaction to Son's humane and friendly greeting of "Hi," a greeting that at once establishes a bond and an equality between the two men. Seemingly, Son's "Hi" strips Sydney of his status as head African, and not until Son begins calling Sydney "Sir" and "Mr. Childs" does the older man begin to communicate with the younger.

Morrison's most intricate exploration of the African petty bourgeois is reserved for Jadine, not Sydney and Ondine. Significantly called Copper Venus, Jadine is a brown white woman, a Europeanized African, an art history graduate of the Sorbonne, an expert on cloisonné, and a cover model for *Elle*. She is one of the tar babies of the novel, a creation of capitalist America.[17] Her behavioral patterns, dress, language, associations, and ideology are all those of the ruling class and, as such, demonstrate her hatred of Africa and all that is associated with it. "To roam around Europe . . . following soccer games" is her goal in life; her fiance is a wealthy European Parisienne who will bring her wealth and unquestioned status.[18] Not surprisingly, her allegiance is more to the Streets, whom she regards "like family, almost," than to Ondine and Sydney, who slave for her.[19] In fact, except for her aunt and uncle, whom she visits only in troubled times, her acquaintances are all Europeans or Europhiliacs like her. Ideologically, she thinks like the European, and like her aunt and uncle, she embraces the stereotypes of the African, calling Son a raggedy nigger and thinking he is about to rape her. Significantly, Son responds: "Rape: Why you little white girls always think somebody's trying to rape you?"[20]

Not only does Jadine think like a European, but also she thinks she is a European. When Son's presence at L'Arbe de la Croix is discovered, she questions his reason for stealing as if she too owned the house: "It depends on what you want from us." Surprised by her irrational, indeed suicidal, association with the Streets, Son replies: "Us? You call yourself 'us'?"[21] Once this association is made clear, it does not surprise us that Jadine often asssumes the position of adoring daughter to the Streets. At dinnertime, she "poured [Valerian's] wine, offered him a helping of this, a dab of that and smiled when she did not have to."[22] And thinking that Valerian's and Margaret's way of life is normal ("Naturally they bickered and taunted one another. Naturally. Normal, even."),[23] indeed the best there is, she belittles African art and she ridicules Michael's attempt to politicize her as to her Africanness: "Actually we didn't talk; we quarreled. About why I was studying art history at that snotty school instead of—I don't know what. Organizing or something. He said I was abandoning my history. My people."[24]

It is this attempt to be other than herself that causes Jadine's insecurity throughout the novel. As a Europhiliac, she feels threatened by African women who are unashamed of their identity and culture and beautiful not simply because they are, but also because they possess pride and dignity in themselves. The African woman in yellow is an example of one such woman. When Jadine meets her, it is quite significant that Jadine is experiencing one of the happiest times of her life because, as Morrison implies, such happiness can never equal the true happiness felt when one celebrates self. Just chosen for the cover of one of France's most fashionable magazines, courted by "three gorgeous and raucous men," and told that she had passed her orals, Jadine was at her zenith. Yet this, the most important day of her life, is not sufficient to erase the insecurity that lies behind the facade of any one who abandons self—in the African's case, all things associated with Africa. It is for this reason that the woman in yellow—beautiful, self-confident, proud, and dignified—is such a disturbing and haunting image for Jadine:

The vision itself was a woman much too tall. Under her long canary yellow dress Jadine knew there was much too much hip, too much bust. The agency would laugh her out of the lobby, so why was she and everybody else in the store transfixed? The height? The skin like tar against the canary yellow dress? She walked down the aisle as though her many-colored sandals were pressing gold tracks on the floor. Two upsidedown V's were scored into each of her cheeks, her hair was wrapped in a gelee as yellow as her dress. The people in the aisles watched her without embarrassment, with full glances instead of sly ones.[25]

What so mesmerizes Jadine and the others, who we assume are Europeans, is the natural beauty of the African woman in yellow—a beauty based on the African's own unique features, not based on those of another race; a beauty that subconsciously forces Jadine to confront her unnatural, imitative beauty, which comes from distorting self. Isn't it interesting that she studies art history, European art history, instead of natural, untamed art? Clearly, she does not have that "genuine talent in her fingers" that would allow her to paint and draw. Neither does she have that genuine beauty, that confidence in self that would prevent her from destroying her natural self in an effort to become as much like a Eruopean as possible.[26] So, "along with everybody else in the market, Jadine gasped. Just a little. Just a sudden intake of air."[27]

Evidence of Jadine's obsession with European looks and culture and her own repugnance of all things African is apparent in her responses to Son, indeed to anyone and anything that has not been tampered with by the European. For example, her recognition of Son's beauty comes only after he has cut off his dreadlocks and shaved his beard. With them, Son is too African, too unlike the European for Jadine: "In a white shirt unbuttoned at the cuffs and throat, and with a gentle homemade haircut, he was gorgeous. He had preserved his mustache but the kinky beard was gone along with the chain-gang hair."[28] Then, too, her love of the Dominican island is reserved only for the tamed land surrounding L'Arbre des la Croix; the other, dark and untamed land "was the ugly part of the Isle des Chevaliers—the part she averted her eyes from whenever she drove past."[29]

Sharing Valerian's need to control life instead of living it, Jadine persistently holds onto the reins of dark dogs galloping on silver feet and, at first, obstinately refuses love-making with Son ("He wasn't manageable") as a way of controlling her emotions.[30] Interesting enough, this image of dark dogs on silver feet continually associated with Jadine suggests the model's concerted effort to hold back the African that is within. Her continual struggle to keep in check her natural hair is only one example.[31] Until Jadine runs toward self rather than from self, she will never experience the genuine feeling of pride and dignity felt and exuded by the woman in yellow.

In fact, the pervasive image of tar, associated with Jadine throughout the novel, illuminates her lack of self-esteem and, more importantly, serves as a measure of Jadine's consciousness of herself as an African. In a negative respect, tar, the sticky material from which the tar baby is built, is the substance of Jadine; she represents that which is inhuman, built by the European as a trap for other Africans, an artificial lure to tempt them to a Europeanized lifestyle. In a positive respect, serving as a symbol of the Africanness Jadine rejects, tar is that which she must internalize. Without this internalization, Jadine is a mere infant, a (tar) baby in her awareness of herself as an African. Thus, the tar must not merely clothe, but be absorbed; it must be accepted with a full consciousness. Only then, Morrison warns us, does it assume value, beauty, and healing properties. Unfortunately, Jadine never becomes fully aware of herself as an African. Indeed, she does not even want to be associated with anything African, for when she sinks in the dark, wet, sticky, mossy floor of the untamed woods of the Isle des Chevaliers, she struggles to rid herself of the tar-like substance enveloping her; she clings in desperation to a nearby tree rather than "cleave like lovers to caress his bark and finger his ridges. Sway when he sways and shiver with him too."[32]

In fact, Jadine has so absorbed the capitalist values of making money and acquiring status that she is ignorant of the traditional African principles that have ensured the survival of African people despite their dehumanized conditions. Unequipped with a sense of humanism, collectivism, and egalitarianism to inform and guide her, she allows her aunt and uncle to wait on her, plays daughter to them instead of being daughter to them, and abandons them to the caprices of Valerian, not knowing what their fate might be. When they most need her, she prays that they don't. And she ignores Ondine's wise words that

a girl has to be a daughter first. She have to learn that. And if she never learns how to be a daughter, she can't never learn how to be a woman. I mean a real woman: a woman good enough for a child; good enough for a man—good enough even for the respect of other women.[33]

But why should we expect Jadine, one who shuns all association with the poor and struggling African masses, to stoop to being a real daughter to a cook, a real woman for a son (i.e., Son) or a real sister to an almond (i.e., Alma)? Revealingly, her Christmas gift of high heels for Ondine, a gift that is more suited for Jadine than for her aged, sore-footed aunt, reflects the extent of Jadine's estrangement from the African masses, for if she is unmindful of her aunt's reality (Ondine's "feet were too tender and her ankles too swollen"), she is certainly unaware of those of the masses.[34]

Unlike Jadine, Son reflects a people-class mentality. He possesses socialist, not capitalist, tendencies. Having learned the principles of humanism, collectivism, and egalitarianism in *Song of Solomon*, he is the Milkman who leaped into the air, stripped of material possessions but clothed with a sense of self: "He had no things to gather—no book of postage stamps, no razor blade or key to any door."[35] Having learned that you cannot fly away and leave a body, the newly conscious Milkman swims away toward the Isle des Chevaliers to struggle for his people. He becomes the Christ-like figure on the L'Arbe des la Croix who saves his people, the revolutionary who politically educates his people, the son, everyone's son—Franklin Green, William Green, Herbert Robinson, Louis Stover—devoid of selfish individualism and conscious of himself as an African.[36] Like a Rastafarian, he comes to D'Arbe des la Croix with dreadlocks, "hair untampered with by man," "living hair" described as "long whips or lashes," "wild, aggressive," "Mau-Mau, Attica, chain-gang hair."[37] The strong, powerful, rebellious hair represents the free-spiritedness, the pride and dignity of the African who has been exploited and oppressed by, but not yet processed by, capitalism. Unfortunately, like a Samson, he leaves D'Arbe des la Croix with cut, processed hair, hair conditioned by the corruptness of the capitalist mentality of Jadine.

Unlike Valerian and Jadine, Son has a sincere love for living things in general, African people in particular, and the African poor especially. He feels at home in natural environments and, as a consequence, is attuned to nature, plucking Valerian's plant to make it bloom and telling Ondine to place banana leaves in her shoes to soothe her sore feet.[38] For the African masses, he has a special love, despite his feelings of "disappointment nudging contempt for the outrage Jade and Sydney and Ondine exhibited in defending property and personnel that did not belong to them from a black man who was one of their own."[39] Unlike Jadine, Sydney, and Ondine, who harbor no love for the struggling African masses, who, in fact, see them as nebulous entities struggling and suffering while they themselves receive only the leftovers of capitalism, Son looks at Gideon and compares this yardman with himself:

> [Yardman] was kneeling, chopping at the trunk of a small tree—while he himself was so spanking clean, clean from the roots of his hair to the crevices between his toes, . . . now he was as near to crying as he'd been since he'd fled from home. . . . "Thanks," whispered Son.[40]

So conscious is Son of the plight of the African masses that on two occasions the overwhelming oppressiveness of their existence brings him close to fainting. The first occasion occurs when he hears the story of the slaves struck blind when they saw Dominique;[41] the second occurs when he realizes the magnitude of the African's self-hatred caused by race and class oppression, a hatred that compels Alma Estee to wear a wig the color of dried blood: "He grew dizzy as soon as he saw her. . . . 'Oh, baby baby baby baby,' he said, and went to her to take off the wig."[42] And when he observes an African sister stripped of all dignity and pride, "word whipping a man on down the street," he is "made miserable by the eyes inside her eyes, and goes to her, arms wide open and says 'Come here.'"[43] Such examples of Son's sincere love for African people are present throughout the novel, revealing his sensitivity to his people's oppression and establishing his position as an African revolutionary in the mold of Garvey, Malcolm, and Nkrumah.[44]

Not only is Son race conscious, but also class conscious. He sees himself as a member of the exploited class, although he himself is not directly exploited: "He saw the things he imagined to be his, including his own reflection, mocked. Appropriated, marketed and trivialized into decor. He could not give up the last thing left to him—fraternity."[45] Clearly, he understands that if African people in general are exploited, then he too is exploited,

that if African people are not free, then he is not free. Nowhere is
his consciousness of himself as a part of the masses more revealing than in the moment he returns to the United States: African
women are crying; African children are mere short people without the vulnerability or laughter associated with them; African
men are either avoiding African women, blinding themselves to
the woman's pain, or becoming African women, having "snipped
off their testicles and pasted them to their chests."[46] If the psy-
chosis of Africans in America is not manifested in either of these
ways, notices Son, it is manifested in a type of Jadism—an aban-
donment of self, brother, and sister to join forces with the oppressor, becoming "black people in whiteface playing black
people in blackface."[47]

With his unobscured race and class consciousness, Son understands that the primary enemy of African people—that is, the
primary cause of the African's plight—is capitalism/imperialism:

> Son's mouth went dry as he watched Valerian chewing a piece of
> ham, his head-of-a-coin profile content, approving even the flavor in
> his mouth although he had been able to dismiss with a flutter of his
> fingers the people whose sugar and cocoa had allowed him to grow
> old in regal comfort; . . . he turned it into candy, . . . and sold it to
> other children and made a fortune . . . and buil[t] a palace with more
> of their labor and then hire[d] them to do more of the work he was not
> capable of and pay them again according to some scale of value that
> would outrage Satan himself.[48]

This passage substantiates Son's class-sightedness. He knows
that it is the African's land and labor, not his skin color, that
primarily results in his exploitation. It is the African's skin color
that facilitates, not causes, his exploitation. Too, he understands
that the United States is the capitalist captial of the world and,
therefore, the African's worst enemy: "When he thought of America, he thought of the tongue that Mexican drew in Uncle Sam's
mouth: a map of the U.S. as an ill-shaped tongue ringed by teeth
and crammed with the corpses of children."[49]

Conscious of both the plight of the African and the cause of
this plight, Son attempts to launch a political education cam-
paign with his primary target being Jadine and his indirect target,
the entire Street household. In his presence, lies are uncovered;
aspirations are revealed; confessions are made. Perhaps the best

example of Son's Christ-like knack for extracting confessions occurs, appropriately enough, during Christmas dinner—in a sense the last supper, in which old myths prevail. It is during this occasion that Valerian reveals his true capitalist nature by firing Gideon and Therese for stealing a few apples while he himself has stolen both their land and their labor, and by responding to Sydney and Ondine as mere servants despite the fact that they have lived with him, and for him, for thirty years. It is also during this occasion that Ondine reveals the secret of Margaret's mutilation of baby Michael and Ondine's own playmothering of him. But most significant for Son and for us is Jadine's revelation of her unequivocal ruling class aspirations, her petty bourgeois tendencies, for while Valerian abuses all present—including her aunt and uncle—she "had defended him. Poured his wine, offered him a helping of this, a dab of that and smiled when she did not have to" as if he were Christ Himself at the Last Supper.[50]

It is because she so blindly accepts the capitalist lifestyle and, more importantly, because Son so ardently loves her that Jadine becomes Son's main target for political education. Significantly, Morrison makes Son a wife/woman killer: He attempts to kill Jadine's old capitalist-class affiliations and instill new people-oriented ones. And while he never gets her to forsake her capitalist ideology, Son does help Jadine become more conscious of herself as an African, largely because he, like the woman in yellow, excudes a pride and dignity in his Africanness.

The first indication of her self-rumination is Jadine's thoughts about the game she has to play with Europeans in order "to make it": "She needed only to be stunning and to convince them she was not as smart as they were. Say the obvious, ask stupid questions, laugh with abandon, look interested, and light up at any display of their humanity if they showed it."[51] A second indication is Jadine's questions about her past and future: "Work? At what? Marriage? Work and Marriage? Where? Who? What can I do with this degree? Do I really want to be a model?"[52] For Jadine, as with most of Morrison's protagonists, the act of questioning signals a psychological maturation, an increased consciousness that is reflected in Jadine's relationship with Margaret: "Any minute now, Margaret would be reaching out her hand and saying 'What'd ja do to yer hay—er? What'd ja do to yer hay—er?' like white girls all over the world, or telling her about Dorcus, the one black girl she ever looked in the face."[53] This increased consciousness is noticeable in her language pattern as well. To Son, when she thinks he will make love to her if they sleep together, she says: "You're going to meddle me and all I want is rest."[54]

But these are little, convenient changes for Jadine. They do not require her to commit class suicide by forsaking her lifestyle. Jadine resists any efforts on Son's part to sensitize her to a more mass way of life. Her resistence is symbolized in her struggle to free herself from the swamp pitch of the Isle des Chevaliers, a physical struggle that reflects her psychological struggle to ward off any significant ideological change: "She twisted with a giant effort around to the road side of the tree—the part of the trunk that leaned out of solid ground."[55] Of course, the "road side" is the Street side, the solid ground, the right of way (the right way), the way of life to which she had become accustomed. And if either Son or Morrison's readers harbor hopes that Jadine is undergoing an ideological renaissance, those hopes are quickly dashed in light of her response to being back in New York. It is a reaction just the opposite of Son's, for whereas he is in tune with the devastating plight of the African people there, she responds to its material convenience, its personal benefits for her: "If ever there was a black woman's town, New York was it."[56] Of course, she is referring to African women like herself, petty bourgeois African women, because for women like Nommo, for the masses of African women, New York is hell. It is the place where all the negativisms of capitalism converge and blossom. It is, in fact, symbolic of the capitalist world, reflecting the two extremes of capitalism—the poor, struggling African masses and the rich European finance bankers and corporate magnates. Here, Jadine can wallow in selfishness. And she does. Son becomes "her fine frame, her stag, her man," a show piece for her friends. Here, Jadine can consume all the delicacies and experience all the sensations of bourgeois life, "eat bean pie on 135th Street, paella on Eight-first Street; . . . eat yogurt on the steps of the Forty-second Street library; listen to RVR and BLS, buy mugs in Azuma's, chocolate chip cookies in Grand Central Station"—in fact, live the life of the Streets.[57]

Since Jadine loves New York, it is not surprising that she hates Son's Eden, Eloe. It is just the opposite of New York. In Eloe,

Jadine's capitalist lifestyle is crystallized. She acts like a typical European tourist, taking the people's pictures and insulting them, like Sula, by sleeping naked in full view of the Eloeans. Moreover, because she has long associated with Europeans more than with Africans, her ways are, in fact, more European than African. For instance, she neither understands nor speaks the Eloean's language, down-home English. In fact, figuratively and literally, Eloe is the blackest thing she ever saw: "She might as well have been in a cave, a grave, the dark womb of earth, suffocating."[58] Indeed, it, and by extension Son, is too black, too much like Africa and its culture for Jadine. She can upbraid Margaret for Margaret's stereotyping and ignorance of the African masses, but Jadine herself adamantly refuses to become a part of the masses. She refuses to become or even, what might be more reasonable, to extract the positive from the African women who come to her in the Eloe night, who pull out a baby-sucked tit and show it to her. She does not have to repeat the destiny of these women but to learn from it. However, for Jadine, like for Sula, these women "were all out to get her, tie her, bind her. Grab the person she had worked hard to become and choke it off with their soft loose tits."[59] Thus, her willingness to share her life with Son, an African man attuned to his culture, becomes contingent upon his willingness to change, his willingness to embrace the capitalist ideology that she holds so dear: "He needed a job, a degree. . . . He should enroll in business school."[60] And it is not any job or any degree; Jadine wants Son to become a lawyer. For, in the long run, happiness with Son is preconditioned by his status and wealth, not the love and happiness she feels in his presence. This is true despite the unhappiness and the psychological disorientation she perceives in the lives of the Streets. And because she opts for human, woman-made products over natural ones, she recognizes both the inner and the outer beauty of Son only after he has discarded his outer Africanness— cut his dreadlocks (hair that is "definitely alive. Left alone and untended it was like foliage and from a distance it looked like nothing less than the crown of a deciduous tree") and put on Valerian's three-piece suit.[61] She accepts him only if he allows her to remake him into an acceptable product of capitalist America, stamped *Made in the U.S.A.*

Kwame Ture once stated that either you are a part of the

problem or a part of the solution. What he meant was that as an
African you can either identify with and struggle for the oppressor or you can identify with and struggle for the oppressed.
And because the oppressor and the oppressed have opposing,
antagonistic interests, to do both is impossible. From the moment that Jadine and Son meet, we are aware that the relationship
between them is antagonistic, for Jadine struggles in behalf of the
interests of the ruling class; Son struggles in behalf of those of the
people class. Since these interests are diametrically opposed,
their relationship can only survive if one of them commits class
suicide by shedding old interests for new ones. It is Son's hope
that he can make Jadine so conscious of the plight of her people
that she will see the vicious nature of capitalism and, thus,
commit class suicide. Just the opposite is true. Son is so mes-
merized by Jadine and so surrounded by ruling class interests
that he is corrupted by the capitalist lifestyle:

> He had it straight before: the pie ladies and the six-string banjo and
> then he was seduced, corrupted by cloisonne and raw silk and the
> color of honey and he was willing to change, to love the cloisonne, to
> abandon the pie ladies and the nickel nickelodeon and Eloe itself.[62]

He becomes the rabbit entrapped by the tar baby that is Jadine.[63]

In fact, from the novel's beginning, there are clues that Son, not
Jadine, will be the one to commit class suicide. First, it is Jadine
who is surrounded by ideological reinforcements; she is surrounded by the lifestyle, the values, the food, the clothes, and the
language and behavioral patterns of the Streets. Son, a loner,
struggles to take Jadine to a higher level, a new state of awareness
in regard to African people while in the midst of capitalist
surroundings. Second, and consequently, it is Son who changes
his dress habits to those of his oppressor. Jadine, sometimes
wearing a seal-skin coat, skin-tight jeans, or a Cheech and Chong
T-shirt, never once clothes herself in the geleelike garb of the
African masses. Third, and most important, Son is not equipped
to change Jadine's consciousness, for, despite his good inten-
tions, his solution, his new and better society, his alternative to
the capitalist way of life, is a return to African traditionalism as
represented by Eloe.[64] Not until Jadine leaves him, opting for

cloisonne rather than Son, does he begin to realize the utopian
nature of his solution:

> Out came the photos [Jadine] had taken in the middle of the road in
> Eloe. Beatrice, pretty Beatrice, Soldier's daughter. She looked stupid.
> Ellen, sweet cookie-faced Ellen, the one he always thought so pretty.
> She looked stupid. They all looked stupid, backwoodsy, dumb,
> dead.[65]

Eloe is a backwoodsy community, largely illiterate and certainly economically underdeveloped. After experiencing the exploitive systems of slavery, colonialsim, neocolonialsim, and
domestic colonialism, and after being exposed to the ideologies
associated with the teachings of Islam and Christianity, neither
Son, Jadine, nor African people in general can return to this past,
highly romanticized way of life. In the words of Aimé Césaire, "If
the African . . . were merely to copy his past, failure would be the
inevitable result."[66] Instead of a return to woebegone days, Son
and Jadine in particular and all African people in general must
extract the positive from traditional Africa and modern capitalism with Africa as the center in order to forge a new society.[67]
Eloe, with all of its positive elements—humanism, collectivism,
and egalitarianism—has its negative characteristics: it is a poor,
underdeveloped, uneducated community.[68] Unfortunately, when
Son does realize the inadequacy of his solution, he does not try
to replace it with a more realistic one. Instead, he willingly
forsakes his role as revolutionary and chases Jadine to share hers
as reactionary. In this respect, he resembles the blind horsemen
who, so devastated by their transition from freedom to slavery,
gave up on life by blinding themselves to their oppressive environment. Son's association with these blind men are made from
our first introduction to him. Gideon and Therese have always
referred to him as the rider or the horseman.[69] Moreover, Therese
"had seen him in a dream smiling at her as he rode away wet and
naked on a stallion."[70]

Once again, Toni Morrison creates an unsatisfactory ending,
despite her new awareness that the primary cause of the plight of
African people is capitalism and despite her knowledge that a
return to a past way of life is impractical. Once again, her protagonist escapes reality, this time by blinding himself to the role

he must play in liberating African people: "Looking neither to the left nor to the right. Lickety-split. Lickety-split. Lickety-lickety-lickety-split."[71]

As with her previous novels, the structure of *Tar Baby* is dialectically related to the thematic development of her canon. It is testimony to Toni Morrison's increased class consciousness. Certainly, it is not by accident that the narrative form in this work is more socialist in nature since in the work she reveals her awareness of the selfish individualism promoted by capitalism and its devastating effects on African people. So, just as Morrison searches thematically for a viable solution to the problem of having a system whereby a few people exploit the majority, she searches structurally for an artistic form, a system that will allow her characters to participate equally in the telling of the story. What is interesting is that while she ignores such a thematic solution, she embraces it structurally. There is not one single narrative voice in the novel but many, each belonging to a major character and each contributing to the universal truth of the work. And while there is an omniscient narrator, it serves merely as the glue to solidify the novel's disparate narrative voices, a type of central committee that consolidates, but does not override, the decisions of its democratic body.

Chapter 2 serves as a significant example of Morrison's restricted use of the omniscient narrator. Intent on presenting an unbiased picture of the petty bourgeois mentality, Morrison has her narrator move systematically from the telling of Jadine's story to Valerian's and, finally, to Margaret's. However, in its presentation, this all-knowing narrator does little more than describe the actions of the characters ("a young woman barely twenty-five years old is wide-awake"), state some obvious, undisputed fact ("A house of sleeping humans is both closed and wide open"), or relate a past event (Jadine's confrontation with the woman in yellow). In Chapter 4 Morrison uses a different but just as successful method of limiting the role of the omniscient narrator. She employs a product of nature, emperor butterflies, as unifying principle. In allowing these butterflies to serve as thread, weaving together all the disparate narrative statements, Morrison, on the one hand, is able to shift her focus from the introduction of the chapter to Margaret Street's need for love and security:

So mulled the occupants of L'Arbe de la Croix that noon the day after a man with living hair stayed for dinner. Outwardly, everything looked the same. Only the emperor butterflies appeared excited about something. Such vigorous flapping in blazing heat was uncommon for them. They hovered near the bedroom windows but the shutters had remained closed all morning and none of them could see a thing. They knew, however, that the woman was in there. Her blue-if-it's-a-boy blue eyes red-rimmed with longing for a trailer softened by columbine and for her Ma.[72]

In this instance, the utilization of the butterflies in addition to the voice of the omniscient narrator creates a text that is as unbiased as possible. For apparently it is the butterflies—just as much a part of nature as humankind—that peer in the windows of the major characters, not some supernatural, omnipotent creation of the author. Moreover, in employing them she creates a more objective work of art, for they force a chasm between the omniscient narrator and the characters, stripping the text of any unnatural interference between character and audience and conveying the impression that the readers are seeing, hearing, and understanding the characters for themselves, that is, participating in the world of the novel.[73]

Another structural example of Morrison's heightened consciousness of the role of capitalism is her organization of the chapters in the novel. Although there are no words to signal divisions in the novel, *Tar Baby* is divided into two parts, both of which are dialectically related to Morrison's most conscious protagonist, Son: BC (before the coming of a new consciousness, i.e., Son) and AD (after the death of the old consciousness). For certainly the Street household is a more conscious one after Son arrives. Ondine's comment that things have changed since the coming of Son is indeed true. In fact, his presence turns the household topsy turvey, replacing myths with truths. All in all, it is quite significant that Morrison arranges her text around her most conscious, indeed Christ-like character, for it is Frank G. Green, alias Son, who is trusted most to be as naturally frank as possible. He is every African's son—every African man, woman, and child—and as such his authenticity is assured.[74]

Perhaps the most important revelation of Toni Morrison's increased class consciousness in regard to structure is her use of clear, concise literal diction throughout the text. In *Tar Baby* Morrison has discarded the intricate writing style that characterizes *Song of Solomon*, a style which reminds the reader of the writings of those African intellectuals who try to emulate the complexity of some of their European counterparts. The complex symbolism and the pervasive mysticism, impressive as they are, are refreshingly absent from his work. Her use of crisp and lucid language patterns to render her tale reflects her determination to create a story that is readable for all audience levels, mass as well as petty bourgeois. As well, her style reveals that she has more of a commitment to discover a solution to the African's plight than to impress her critics with her dexterity in using the English language.

Structurally as well as thematically, Morrison reflects her heightened consciousness in *Tar Baby*. Unfortunately, this increased awareness is not sufficient to enable her to propose a viable solution for eradicating the plight of African people—a unified African people who control their own destiny, who see Africa at the core of their existence, who abide by the principles of humanism, collectivism, and egalitarianism, and who extract and utilize only those positive elements from traditional African culture as well as other cultures. Fortunately, with *Beloved*, it seems as if Morrison has digested the ideas posited in *Tar Baby* because for the first time, she proposes the fundamental part of a solution to the African's nation-class oppression: African solidarity.

6
Beloved
Solidarity as Solution

One people, one struggle, one solution—this is the theme of Toni Morrison's fifth, most conscious novel to date. In her four earlier works—*The Bluest Eye, Sula, Song of Solomon,* and *Tar Baby*—Morrison demonstrates a keen awareness of, concern for, and dedication to African people. Like a scientist, she uses each work as a laboratory in which to research a hypothesis as to the nature of the oppression experienced by African people and to posit a solution to it. Starting with the issue of race as our primary form of oppression (*The Bluest Eye*), next demonstrating that a person alone is only half a person (*Sula*), adding the problem of class exploitation to that of race (*Song of Solomon*), and then refining that idea in recognition of capitalism/imperialism as the primary target against which we must struggle (*Tar Baby*), Toni Morrison uses *Beloved* as a vehicle in which to propose solidarity as the only viable solution possible for African people.

The ambivalent, uncommittal endings of the first four novels and the clear, confident ending of *Beloved* can be used as examples to gauge the author's own developing consciousness in regard to both the nature of the African's oppression and the solution.[1] *The Bluest Eye* ends with the demise of the main character: Pecola Breedlove becomes a mentally unstable twelve-year-old who has miscarried her sister and her child. *Sula,* twelve years old when Morrison's second novel begins and thirty years old when she dies, prefers selfish individualism, which brings death, over individuality with social responsibility, which brings life. In *Song of Solomon* Milkman, having gained consciousness about himself and his people, flies away instead of passing on this political consciousness. In *Tar Baby,* a conscious, socialist-oriented Son tries unsuccessfully to politically educate the selfish, capitalist-oriented Jadine. His failure to do so is in part due to his own seduction by the capitalist way of life. Ultimately, he runs off to the briar patch as did the blind horsemen and as do the burnt-out revolutionaries.

While each of these novels concentrates on a different but related factor in the oppression of African people, all are symbiotically related. In fact, each serves as a stepping stone that enables Morrison to move to the next level of discovery. For example, in Morrison's novels each character is a development of the preceding one: The twelve-year old Pecola becomes the twelve-year old Sula; the thirty-year old Sula becomes the thirty-one year old Milkman; the conscious Milkman who flies away unburdened by the material objects of the capitalist world (i.e., the heavy tail of the peacock) becomes the Son who unemcumbered and single-handedly tries to politically educate the people of L'Arbre de la Croix; the unsuccessful Son becomes the Paul D who defies defeat by returning again and again to struggle for his people. Significantly, Paul D is part of a struggling collective.

But while these novels are developmental, pursuing the answer to one question in building-block fashion, there are observable qualitative differences. Just as *Song of Solomon*, in theme and in structure, represents a dialectical change, indeed a categorical conversion, in Toni Morrison's consciousness of herself as a part of the oppressed nation of African people, *Beloved* marks another leap in Morrison's consciousness. It is her goal in this work to demonstrate to her reader (always an African audience) that collectivism is only the first step in eradicating the national oppression and class exploitation of African people. Although never primary until this work, the intrinsic value of collectivism to the African community has always been a part of the Morrisonian canon. The use of bird and flight symbolism in most of her novels reveals the author's belief in that value. In *Sula* Morrison chooses robins—birds of harmony and unity—to portend the protagonist's return to the Bottom and her effect on that community. In *Song of Solomon*, the peacock represents unity, containing all of the colors of the world, as it does worldly goods.

Just as crucial, the suicidal or homocidal nature of those Africans who divorce themselves from other Africans has also been a recurring theme.[2] Such characters as Geraldine and Soaphead Church in *The Bluest Eye*, Sula, Macon Dead, Jr., and the unconscious Milkman of *Song of Solomon*, Sydney, Ondine, and Jadine of *Tar Baby*—all demonstrate some unnatural, suicidal, or perverted characteristics that are often illegal and always genocidal for the African community. In an interview with Thomas LeClair, Morrison uses such terms as *village* and *tribe* to make clear her belief in an organic, Pan-African view of the race:

> I write what I have recently begun to call village literature, fiction that is really for the village, for the tribe. Peasant literature for my people, which is necessary and legitimate. . . . My work bears witness and suggests who the outlaws were, who survived under what circumstances and why, what was legal in the community as opposed to what was legal outside it. . . . My people are being devoured.[3]

To show them the historical truth that collective struggle is the only practical solution for African people, Morrison writes a historical novel, one that explores the most oppressed period in the history of African people: slavery. By doing so, she demonstrates her clear understanding that conditions that existed then are not significantly different from those which confront African people today. That is, because Africans are faced with circumstances equally oppressive and genocidal as those in slavery, Toni Morrison shows them the life-saving benefits of uniting as one to confront a common enemy, the same enemy they struggled against more than one hundred years ago: capitalism. Certainly she has come to understand that "capitalism is but the gentleman's form of slavery."[4] Stated differently, the message conveyed in *Beloved* is as follows: No longer should African people be physically intimidated by Europeans as in *The Bluest Eye*; no longer should African people indulge in the selfish individualism of *Sula*; no longer should African people ignore their duty to pass on the knowledge of their history as in *Song of Solomon*; and no longer should African people attempt to wage struggle alone and, thus, unsuccessfully as in *Tar Baby*. Solidarity, the theme of *Beloved*, is the solution for African people.

As in previous works, Morrison's thematic astuteness is reflected in her narrative structure. In *Beloved*, on the one hand, she creates a text unencumbered by symbols indicating divisions and defiant of the linear tradition of the Western world in order to create in form what she does in substance: the qualitatively unchanged status of African people. On the other hand, she creates such a text in order to point to our solution: collectivism. To crystallize the dire necessity of collective action to the survival of African people, Morrison juxtaposes isolated struggle with collective struggle and selfish individualism with individualism conditioned by social responsibility. In *Beloved*, most forms of isolation are genocidal for the race. Denver's isolation in life, 124's isolation in the community, and Beloved's isolation in death all serve to further divide the African community and, as a consequence, leave it vulnerable to the oppression and exploitation of the slave society. For instance, when Baby Suggs labors alone to feed the community, she insults it:

> Too much, they thought. Where does she get it all, Baby Suggs, holy? . . . and loving everybody like it was her job and hers alone. . . . Loaves of bread and fishes were His powers.[5]

Since it is usually best for all that individual needs and desires be conditioned by those of the collective, Baby Suggs's self-oriented behavior is tantamount to heresy. Indeed, the repercussions of this God-like action—this attempt to do alone that which should be done together—is felt for two generations. For the community, in spite, refuses to warn Baby Suggs that slave trappers are approaching, setting in motion the conditions under which Sethe murders Beloved:

> The good news . . . was that Halle got married and had a baby coming. [Baby Suggs] fixed on that and her own brand of preaching, having made up her mind about what to do with the heart that started beating the minute she crossed the Ohio River. And it worked out, worked out just fine, until she got proud and let herself be overwhelmed by the sight of her daughter-in-law and Halle's children— one of whom was born on the way—and have a celebration of blackberries that put Christmas to shame. Now she stood in the garden smelling disapproval, feeling a dark and coming thing, and seeing high-topped shoes that she didn't like the look of at all. At all.[6]

Interestingly enough, Beloved becomes the symbol by which African people are to measure the devastating effect of isolation—self-imposed or forced. Isolation literally tears apart the family—the nuclear, the extended, and the nation. The personification of isolation and all things inherent in it, including selfish individualism, greed, and destruction, Beloved succeeds in dividing 124 from the rest of the African community. It is she who drives Howard and Burglar from home—"as soon as merely looking in a mirror shattered it (that was the signal for Burglar); as soon as two tiny hand prints appeared in the cake (that was it for Howard)."[7] It is she who separates Paul D, Sethe, and Denver just when their three shadows were holding hands and just when they were erecting bonds with the African community:

> Paul D made a few acquaintances; spoke to them about what work he might find. Sethe returned the smiles she got. Denver was swaying with delight. And on the way home, although leading them now, the shadows of three people still held hands.[8]

Not until the cause of the separation is clarified, is out in the open, struggled with and struggled against, can African people come together again. Beloved must materialize into a visible, tangible entity of which the community is aware, instead of an amorphous apparition, an oppression of which the community is unconscious. Paul D gives this apparition substance; he is the Son who does not give up but returns to struggle again and again, the Malcolm who teaches his people the value of struggle.[9] His presence sets in motion the necessary purgative confrontation between Sethe, Beloved, and the Cincinnati African community. Significantly, when he comes, "Things became what they were," not what Sethe and the African community imagined.[10] Once the enemy is identified, once it is out in the open, the community struggles collectively against that which divides them. And it is only through the collective will and action of the people that Beloved, the enemy, dies: "Unloaded, 124 is just another weathered house needing repair."[11] By and by, all trace of Beloved is gone. She is not even remembered by those "who had spoken to her, lived with her, fallen in love with her."[12]

Thus, the stress on shared relationships, community, and race responsibilty—the traditional African priniciple of collectivism—is the dominant theme of the novel. In *Beloved* life is hell, but togetherness, shared experience, and brotherly/sisterly love help the characters to survive, if not to forge better lives for themselves. This emphasis on social responsibility, the unselfish devotion of Africans helping other Africans, makes *Beloved* Toni Morrison's most conscious novel to date.

Stamp Paid, Baby Suggs, and Hi Man are examples of Africans who have struggled to internalize the principle of collectivism and who—through their theory and practice—struggle to set the example for other Africans to follow. Deciding that he and other slaves had paid more than enough already for whatever had come in life and whatever was to come, Stamp Paid extends a debt-lessness to other Africans "by helping them pay out and off whatever they owed in misery. Beaten runaways? He ferried them and rendered them paid for; gave them their bill of sale, so to speak."[13] For this unselfish dedication to his people, he is wel-comed in the houses of Africans throughout the community. Always. Although Baby Suggs "forgets" the necessity of collec-tive responsibility in celebrating her daughter-in-law's safe ar-rival out of slavery, her actions overall are characterized by a selflessness. Bought out of slavery by her son Halle, she becomes an unchurched preacher, dedicating her life to loving African people and encouraging them to love themselves:

> Here in this place, we flesh; flesh that weeps, laughs; flesh that dances on bare feet in grass. Love it. Love it hard. Yonder they do not love your flesh. They despise it. They don't love your eyes; they'd just as soon pick em out. No more do they love the skin on your back. Yonder they flay it. And O my people they do not love your hands. Those they only use, tie, bind, chop off and leave empty. Love your hands! Love them. Raise them up and kiss them. Touch others with them. . . . *You* got to love it, you![14]

Baby Suggs's sermons in the clearing are political education sessions in which she clarifies the roles of oppressor and op-pressed. The oppressor has no love for the oppressed; the op-pressed must love themselves and one another.

In the spirit of the flying African of the Virginia Hamilton myth, Hi Man takes the responsibility for the collective.[15] One more experienced with the hardships of slave existence, he teaches other Africans that "a man could risk his own life, but not his brother's." And, most important, he teaches that all must be freed from oppression or none, "one lost, all lost." This lesson is begun in *Song of Solomon*, learned in *Tar Baby*, and acted out in *Beloved*. Focusing on the postslavery convict lease system, Morrison uses the chain as a literal symbol of the spiritual link (i.e., the faith and trust) necessary between African people:

"They trusted the rain and the dark, yes, but mostly Hi Man and each other."[16] This kind of bond between African people is not found in any other work by Morrison. It is the kind of bond that she hopes will once again exist between African people.

Crucial in her exploration of the collective solution to the African's oppression is the slave setting, for it serves to enhance the theme of *Beloved* by pointing up the dialectical relationship between problem and solution: that the solution to the problem arises from the condition (or conditions) that creates it. Simultaneously, Morrison's setting had to be one in which the strategy for solving the problem was not only clearly evident but also inevitable. For she understands that the solution then is the solution now.[17] The most skillful method of unveiling this truth is by choosing a historical period in which the African's primary enemy, capitalism, is unobscured by its secondary and consequential effects: race and gender oppression. In *Beloved*, gender oppression is not a visible problem that exists between African men and women, but it is one that exists within the context of the economic relationship between master and slave, and race is only a later justification for the oppression of African people.[18] Clearly, then, Morrison's choice of setting is germane in crystallizing the nature of the African's oppression, for the economic source of both race and gender oppression is unobscured in slavery.

Refreshingly, the relationship between African men and women is generally positive. Paul D is the Son who returns to the struggle, wiser and more committed. In regard to women, he is characterized as a man who has never mistreated a woman in his life and as a man who is grateful to women for his life.[19] He is described as Christ-like on occasion, at least in his manner toward women: "There was something blessed in his manner. Women saw him and wanted to weep—to tell him that their chest hurt and their knees did too."[20] Not long after he sees Sethe for the first time in many years, "He rubbed his cheek on her back and learned that way her sorrow, the roots of it; its wide trunk and intricate branches."[21] It is his presence at 124 Bluestone that forces the necessary purgative confrontation between Sethe, the community, and Beloved. When he becomes a part of the household, "Things became what they were."[22] He is, in fact, the only major male protagonist in the Morrisonian canon who has a positive relationship with a female and, furthermore, who struggles with a female to forge this positive relationship.[23] He believes that "only this woman Sethe could have left him his manhood like that. He wants to put his story next to hers."[24]

It is a mark of Toni Morrison's heightened consciousness that she depicts the life that Paul D struggles to build with Sethe as one based on a common history and a common struggle that both shared on Sweet Home. It is not based on sex, such as the Milkman-Sweet affair of *Song of Solomon*, nor based on physical appearance, such as the Son-Jadine affair of *Tar Baby*. Unlike Copper Venus, Sethe is the woman in yellow, an African woman, chokeberry tree and all. She is satisfied with the real happiness love brings, not with the artificial contentment bought by status and wealth:

> Perhaps it was the smile, or maybe the ever-ready love she saw in his eyes—easy and upfront, the way colts, evangelists and children look at you: with love you don't have to deserve—that made her go ahead and tell him what she had not told Baby Suggs, the only person she felt obliged to explain anything to.[25]

Together, Paul D and Sethe must struggle to forge a positive life under the most oppressing conditions. And, of course, since the novel is to serve as a lesson for her people, the same struggle must be waged between African men and women today.[26]

Like gender oppression, race oppression is examined as a consequence of the economic exploitation of African people. The thesis of Eric Williams's *Capitalism and Slavery* is threefold: that the economic demands of the budding capitalist nations led to the slave trade and slavery; that the African was enslaved primarily as a consequence of this demand (i.e., because he was a good agricultural worker, not because he was an African); and that out of the need to justify the enslavement of human beings, these nations institutionalized racism. According to him, "Slavery was not born of racism: rather, racism was the consequence of slavery."[27] Toni Morrison seems in agreement with Williams's thesis, for *Beloved*—while revealing that today African people are oppressed equally because of the color of their skin and their poverty—clearly proves that race was a later justification for the enslavement of African people.

To accomplish her goal of clarifying the dialectical relationship between race oppression and class exploitation, Morrison—as do Williams and others—documents history by showing that the European and the Native American Indian were enslaved before the African.[28] The European slave (indentured servant) is represented by Miss Amy Denver of Boston. According to Denver, "My mama worked for these here people to pay for her passage. But then she had me and since she died right after, well, they said I had to work for em to pay it off."[29] The parallels between her experiences and those of Africans are similar. Her mother is dead and her father, unknown—perhaps the slavemaster. She shared the same work experience and punishment as those of Africans: "I used to be a good size. Nice arms and everything. Wouldn't think it, would you? That was before they put me in the root cellar."[30] She too is denied education, making her English vernacular almost indistinguishable from that of the African slave: "Be so pretty on me" and "Mr. Buddy whipped my tail." Of course, the significant difference between the two is skin color. Amy can and does run away from the slave plantation to blend in with other Europeans in Boston. Thus, while a runaway slave herself, it is quite significant that Amy is capable of saying: "[I] wouldn't be caught dead in daylight with an African runaway."[31] This difference in skin color, according to both the economic historian Eric Williams and the historic novelist Toni Morrison, was for the capitalists the overwhelming economic motivation for securing a non-European slave population.

The Native American Indian was a better alternative for that reason. However, as Morrison documents, the Indians soon proved disadvantageous as well. Weakened by labor exploitation and the European's diseases, millions of Indians sickened and died. The genocidal effects of slavery on the Indian is clearly documented in the following passage from *Beloved:*

In between that calamity and this, they had visited George III in London, published a newspaper, made baskets, led Oglethorpe through forests, helped Andrew Jackson fight Creek, cooked maize, drawn up a constitution, petitioned the King of Spain, been experimented on by Dartmouth, established asylums, wrote their language, resisted settlers . . . All to no avail. The forced move to the Arkansas river, insisted upon by the same president they fought for against the

Creek, destroyed another quarter of their already shattered
number. . . . The disease they suffered now was a mere inconve-
nience compared to the devastation they remembered.[32]

Also clearly documented is the bond forged between the African
and the Indian based on their common oppression. Accurately,
Morrison shows the Indian's willingness to make a home for
runaway African slaves, allowing them to become a part of the
tribe or to leave as they pleased:

Buffalo men, they [the Indians] called them [the runaway slaves] . . .
Nobody from a box in Alfred, Georgia, cared about the illness the
Cherokee warned them about, so they stayed, all forty-six, resting,
planning their next move. Paul D had no idea of what to do and knew
less than anybody it seemed. He heard his co-convicts talk knowl-
edgeably of rivers and states, towns and territories. Heard Cherokee
men describe the beginning of the world and its end. Listened to tales
of other Buffalo men they knew—three of whom were in the healthy
camp a few miles away. Hi Man wanted to join them; others wanted to
join him. Some wanted to leave; some to stay on.[33]

The primary enemy of all three groups—the exploited European
indentured servant, the Native American Indian, and the African—was and is capitalism. First the theft of raw materials for
developing industrial countries and then the theft of a labor force
to work within these countries gave birth to notions of inferiority
and superiority that would lead to race and gender oppression.
According to Walter Rodney,

The simple fact is that no people can enslave another for centuries
without coming out with a notion of superiority, and when the colour
and other physical traits of those peoples were quite different it was
inevitable that the prejudice should take a racist form.[34]

Of course, Morrison is most interested in documenting the
history of the African in slavery. And in so doing she is at her
best. Slavery, and its aftermath, come to life for the reader. First,
all the history that the reader has learned about slavery is
sketched out on a giant canvas: the separation of women and
children from men; the treatment of slaves—both male and
female, children and adults—as beasts of burden; the sexual
exploitation of African women by European men. Like horses,

Paul D and others like him are hitched to wagons with "bits" in their mouths. Like a cow, Sethe is milked by her slavemasters. Women, children, and men are whipped mercilessly. Stamp Paid's wife and Ella become the sexual playthings of the slavemaster. Perhaps the most vicious and cruel of all these acts was the dispersal of the race:

> The last of her [Baby Suggs's] children, whom she had barely glanced at when he was born because it wasn't worth the trouble to learn features you would never see change into adulthood anyway. Seven times she had done that: held a little foot; examined the fat fingertips with her own—fingers she never saw become the male or female hands a mother would recognize anywhere.[35]

And perhaps more important than her skillful way of bringing to life the facts about slavery is Morrison's adeptness at correcting myths about slavery, the foremost of which is that slave life for some was good. Slavery was slavery, on Sweet Home as well as any other plantation. Baby Suggs testifies to this truism when Mr. Garner takes her to the European abolitionists, the Bodwins, after she is bought out of slavery by her son Halle. Mr. Garner's attempts to distinguish himself from the collective of slaveholders is regarded as a hypocritical distinction:

> "Tell em, Jenny [Baby Suggs]. You live any better on any place before mine?"
> "No, sir," she said. "No place. . . ."
> "Ever go hungry?"
> "No, sir. . . ."
> "Did I let Halle buy you or not?"
> "Yes, sir, you did," she said, thinking, But you got my boy and I'm all broke down. You be renting him out to pay for me way after I'm gone to Glory.[36]

Not only were conditions in slavery qualitatively indistinguishable no matter whether you had a "good" master or a "bad" master, but also, in or out of slavery, Baby Suggs reveals that life for her has been one continuous cycle of oppression: "Her past had been like her present—intolerable."[37] For a "free" African living in a slave society, life is not qualitatively different either.

In fact, it is to Morrison's credit that she wants the reader to make no such distinction between slavery, its aftermath, and now. In the 1870s there were "whole towns wiped clean of Negroes; eighty-seven lynchings in one year alone in Kentucky; four colored schools burned to the ground; grown men whipped like children; children whipped like adults; black women raped by the crew; property taken, necks broken."[38] One hundred years later, in the 1970s when *Tar Baby* was written,

> The old people were in kennels and childhood was underground. But why were all the black girls crying on buses, in Red Apple lines, at traffic lights and behind the counters of Chemical Bank. Crying from a grief so stark you would have thought they'd been condemned to death by starvation. . . . It depressed him, all that crying, for it was silent and veiled by plum lipstick and the thin gray lines over their eyes. Who did this to you? Who has done this thing to you? . . . The street was choked with beautiful males who had found the whole business of being black and men at the same time too difficult and so they'd dumped it. They had snipped off their testicles and pasted them to their chests.[39]

With the qualitatively unchanged status of the African, Paul D's cry of desperation and frustration echoes into the present: "How much is a nigger supposed to take? Tell me. How much?"[40] Although Stamp Paid's answer of "All he can" seems pitifully weak in light of the devastating conditions that threaten the survival of a nation of people, it is strengthened by the solution presented in this novel: solidarity. That is, Morrison demonstrates that the African's plight is less harsh and potentially extirpated if it is seen as a collective struggle: "Days of company: knowing the names of forty, fifty other Negroes, their views, habits; where they had been and what done; of feeling their fun and sorrow along with her own, . . . at 124 and in the Clearing, along with the others, she [Sethe] had claimed herself."[41]

Unity: this is the only way African people can survive. It is only when the African, through self or forced isolation, exists outside of the collective that the struggle appears endless and the burden, unbearable. When Baby Suggs (in trying to do all the work of providing for the community by herself) and Sethe (in "trying to do it all alone with her nose in the air") and Africans in general are "resigned to life without aunts, cousins, children"— these are the times when the African's plight is intolerable.[42]

Structurally, Morrison matches form with substance. On the

one hand, the novel's inscription, "Sixty Million and more," at once sets up the conditions with which the reader should analyze the story. Since the emphasis is on the theft of a sizable portion of a nation of people, the reader is prevented from separating one African from another. African people are to be seen as a collective. On the other hand, we are introduced to unmarked chapters throughout a Morrison novel for the first time. The absence of passages, dates, and numbers reflects a negation of time in regard to African people. Moreover, the consistent use of all capital letters for the first few words of each chapter contributes to this sense of timelessness and this feeling of running (i.e., reading) in place. Such a timelessness exists because the conditions under which African people live have remained qualitatively unchanged, reflecting a continual cycle of oppression.

Morrison reinforces her theme of one people, one struggle, one solution in several ways. First, she begins each chapter in the novel's present, then returns to the past in order to bridge the gap between occurrences of the past and those of the present. The chapter beginning on page 114 is an excellent case in point. This chapter details Beloved's systematic efforts to move Paul D out of 124 and out of Sethe's life. It begins with the words "SHE MOVED HIM" and then shifts to the past to cite the methods Beloved uses to do so. Second, the beginnings, since they are often structured as subordinate phrases or clauses, seem more like middles, once again emphasizing the fact that oppression for the African exists as one uninterrupted continuum: "TO GO BACK to the original hunger was impossible."[43] Thus, anywhere along the African's life cycle—the beginning, the middle, the end—conditions are relatively unchanged. The overall message conveyed is that African people end up where they began.

Another skillful structural device that Morrison uses to reflect the unchanging status of African people is the repetition of key words, phrases, or sentences. Sometimes whole chapters take up where the preceding ones left off. On page 209, the chapter ends with the lines: "She's mine, Beloved. She's mine." The next chapter, which begins on page 210, uses a similar sentence construction and utilizes three of the same words: "I AM BELOVED and she is mine."

Pronouns too are used to begin chapters and have the same thematic and structural effect. For instance, by beginning one chapter on page 115 with the pronoun *she*, Morrison creates a textual continuum that has relevance to the uninterrupted oppression of African people.[44]

Arguably, there are other germane reasons for Morrison's creation of unmarked chapters in this work. One example is that they reflect the lack of substantive differences between African people. Not only are Africans worldwide one people having the same history and sharing the same plight (the slave setting is a constant reminder of this shared history and plight), but also because they are a powerless people, they are seen as one ("All niggers look alike") by those outside the African nation, no matter what their class status might be. Significantly, after a novel in which she has explored the class question as it relates to African people—*Tar Baby*—Morrison writes one in which class distinctions do not exist. Clearly, she wants African people to see themselves as one people, undivided by their class status.

Also, unmarked chapters reinforce the theme of *Beloved* by constantly reminding the reader that collective struggle then and now is the only practical way to alleviate the oppression African people experience. Since the people are one, the history is the same, and the plight remains unchanged, clearly the solution is the same.

Other structural devices that bring cohesion to the text and, as a consequence, reflect the oneness that exists among African people, are Morrison's habit of unfolding bits of information about someone or something she has already mentioned and her use of repetition within and between chapters. Before we understand the significance of Amy Denver's life-saving role or even her name, we are introduced to her by the following dependent clause: "And if it hadn't been for that girl looking for velvet."[45] And before we understand to what Paul D is referring, we know his opinion of it: "Maybe shaped like one, but nothing like any tree he knew because trees were inviting."[46]

Within chapters, Morrison uses repetition to achieve structural coherence as well as to reflect, thematically, the African's unchanging reality. The refrain, "It went on that way and might have stayed that way,"[47] helps the reader to perceive the information before and after as elements of one continuum. Moreover, the rhythm of the line, when read aloud, creates a monotone, an unchanging sound that matches an unchanging condition.

Finally, unmarked chapters reflect Morrison's desire to recognize and to embrace a part of African heritage. From the traditional African perspective, time is cyclic, not linear as in Western culture. The past, present, and future merge into one continuum, allowing African people to move forward and backward in time as they please and allowing their "dead" ancestors to remain among them as guiding forces. Both elements of African time are relevant to the theme of *Beloved:* There is no significant difference between the African's past, present, and future, and African people cannot afford to lose forever one more of their own (e.g., Beloved, although dead, is still a part of the Sethe household).

Overall, such skillful techniques as unmarked chapters and refrains unify the narrative structure of *Beloved.* They signify the unity among African people that is plausible and necessary in order to effect a real change. And just as Morrison is adept at reflecting the unity so needed in the African world, so is she skillful in mirroring the disunity that presently exists. The Beloved chapters serve as a case in point.

As thematically Beloved represents isolation, chaos, and disunity in the novel, so structurally the sections in the novel that describe and characterize her thoughts are symbolic of isolation, chaos, and disunity. Her words are out of order, or important words are omitted altogether ("Tell me your earrings"), and her names for things are incorrect ("Your woman [i.e., Sethe] she never fix up your hair?").[48] Words are not capitalized and whole passages are left unpunctuated. Furthermore, when Beloved becomes the dominant force at 124 Bluestone, communication takes on the unnatural form of poetry. The use of poetry as a narrative device simulates the unnatural state of affairs that exists at 124:

Beloved
   You are my sister
   You are my daughter
   You are my face; you are me
   I have found you again, you have come back to me
   You are my Beloved
   You are mine
   You are mine
   You are mine[49]

Moreover, in an effort to rid the community of the presence of Beloved and any thoughts of her, Morrison repeats three times the line, "It was not a story to pass on," a structural technique used to complete or end a thematic concern—Beloved.[50]

After five novels, Toni Morrison comes to terms with both the dilemma confronting African people and a part of the solution that must be embraced by them. The novels make clear the facts that African people suffer from a crisis of the African personality, stemming from our nation-class oppression, that our primary enemy is capitalism in all of its disguises, and that the solution to this crisis lies in collective, not individual, struggle against this enemy. Furthermore, Morrison crystallizes the strategy— political education through communication—which ushers in the solution: collective struggle. For it is the lack of communication that causes the major disasters in the novel: the African community does not warn Baby Suggs and Sethe of the slave trappers' approach ("Not Ella, not John, not anybody ran down or to Bluestone road, to say some new whitefolks with the Look just rode in");[51] Sethe does not tell Denver the reason for her murder of Beloved ("All the time, I'm afraid the thing that happened that made it all right for my [Denver's] mother to kill my sister could happen again");[52] and neither does Sethe ask the community for help once she is released from jail ("She returned their disap- proval with the potent pride of the mistreated").[53] Communica- tion—the sharing of ideas through the Word—creates the unity in the novel: the songs, gestures, and signs of slaves, the word from Hi Man as well as Baby Suggs's speaking of the Word. It is as if Morrison is advising African people to speak the Word of their common history, their common plight, their common struggle, their common destiny. And she matches her theory with practice because it is through her Word that Africans become a more conscious people. So with the words of Stamp Paid all African people say to her: "Listen here, girl, you can't quit the Word. It's given to you to speak. You can't quit the Word."[54] *A luta con- tinua.* The struggle continues.

7

A Rationalization for and an Assessment of Toni Morrison's Developing Class Consciousness

A number of factors contributed to Toni Morrison's developing class consciousness: environment, family background, historical events, her Random House experience, and the writing process itself. Impacting upon her consciousness throughout her life— particularly the years in which she wrote (1965–86)—these factors helped her to become more conscious of the crisis of the African personality, the cause and effects of it, and a fundamental part of the solution needed to address it. However, to state that Morrison's consciousness increased considerably in regard to the African's plight and solution is not to state that she reached full consciousness in regard to them. Crucial questions are left unaddressed in the Morrisonian canon, questions such as the importance of a land base in a people's ability to control their own destiny and the importance of establishing the most expedient and just system of control for that land base. Still, her novels are reflections of her increasing awareness of the nature of the African's dilemma and her increasing commitment to help solve it. Surely, with her keen awareness, sincere commitment, and unwavering persistence, a full, satisfactory solution should be forthcoming.

Morrison's early years in the steel mill town of Lorain, Ohio, during the depression years created within her a sensitivity toward the struggling masses in general and African people in particular. Her father's views were to prove influential in further shaping this sensitivity. He believed that all African people were superior to Europeans because their position in society was a moral one. Like Guitar and Son in particular, he felt that harmony could never exist between the races, a position Morrison admits to having moved closer to later in life as a result of her growing consciousness that racism is an institution entrenched in the fabric of the United States.[1] Thus, Son seems to mouth the words of the author's father when he tells Jadine that Africans and Europeans should not socialize: "They should work together sometimes, but they should not eat together or live together or sleep together. Do any of those personal things in life."[2]

Morrison's mother, like her uncles, challenged segregated laws, both written and unwritten. According to Morrison, "My mother's great thing was to go in theaters on Saturday afternoons and sit where she wished."[3] And her uncles, like those of Maureen Peal, found it easy to file suits against people who refused to serve Africans in ice cream parlors. Moreover, the Morrison house, filled with the women friends of her mother, conjures up images of the social life of African women in Sula's house. Both the fictional and the real were houses in which life was filled with the *word* of the African reality, in which the material world was colored by the spiritual.[4]

Karl Marx, in *The Communist Manifesto*, asks a profound question that has relevance to this discussion: "Does it require deep intuition to comprehend that man's ideas, views, and conceptions, in a word, man's consciousness, changes with every change in the conditions of his material existence, in his social relations and in his social life?"[5] Certainly, the material conditions that affect society in general and African people in particular helped to shape the consciousness of Toni Morrison. The civil rights and black power movements of the 1950s and 1960s were two such events that contributed to the author's developing consciousness.

Toni Morrison's novels document the author's awareness of and concern for the historical conditions that sparked the national struggle of African people against oppression and exploitation. *Song of Solomon* makes specific reference to the brutal death of the fourteen-year-old Emmett Louis "Bobo" Till and to the consequential, justifiable anger and outrage felt by the African community. For whistling at a twenty-one-year old European woman, Till was flogged, mutilated, lynched, shot in the head, and thrown into the Tallahatchie River with "a 70-pound cotton gin fan around his neck." According to Clenora Hudson, "News of the Till incident internationally shocked, horrified, and sobered reasonable minds to the realization that something had to be done about racial injustice in America," and "Till's lynching rapidly grew into the status of a household subject in the African-American community."[6] Significantly, Morrison uses the barbershop, the popular meeting place in the African community, to show the reaction of the African community to Till's death. The racist church bombing of four little African girls in Birmingham, Alabama, had an equal impact on Morrison's consciousness, for it is this event that jettison's Guitar on his quest for money. These two events, and countless others just as reprehensible, must have informed Morrison's consciousness.

It is also noteworthy that during Toni Morrison's tenure as an instructor at Howard University (1957–64), events of significance were occurring in the Washington, D.C., area, and at least one militant campus organization was contributing to these events. The Non-Violent Action Group (NAG), founded at Howard in 1960, was instrumental in desegregating twenty-five facilities in the D.C. area in its first year alone. Moreover, during this year, "One hundred persons were arrested in connection with demonstrations conducted by NAG."[7] Such a conscientious African as Toni Morrison could not have been ignorant of the existence of such an organization nor unmoved by the events credited to it.

Interesting also is that one member of this group, Cleveland Sellars, who was a student at Howard beginning fall 1962, documents having a roommate whose disinterest in racial concerns mirrors that of the unconscious Milkman: " 'Fuck it, man,' he said to me one night in exasperation after I asked him if he didn't feel some responsibility to try to improve racial conditions." The roommate continued by saying, "I'm interested in four things . . . A degree, a good job, a good woman and a good living. That's all." Of course, the documentation of this conversation—quoted in Sellars's book *The River of No Return*—is neither proof of Morrison's knowledge of it, nor proof of her awareness of the book (which was published in 1973, seven years before the publication of *Song of Solomon*), but it does serve as proof of the attitude of many of the students at Howard University during the time that Morrison served as instructor, an attitude of which Morrison was

certainly aware. According to Sellars, "My roommate was typical. Although few stated their feelings so bluntly, most of
Howard's students shared his attitude."[8]

Morrison's years at Random House must also be considered in
understanding her developing consciousness. As an editor for
some of the more significant works written by Africans, she was
exposed to the thoughts of some who were more conscious than
she of the nature of the plight confronting her people. One such
African, Chinweizu, must have had a considerable impact on
her. After editing his work, *The West and the Rest of Us*, Morrison's own works would reflect a qualitative leap in the author's
consciousness, not only of the class and race oppression of Africans, but also of the primacy of class exploitation.

The dialectical connection between the ideas of Morrison and
those of Chinweizu is not as farfetched as it may at first seem.
Since the plight of African people has always been her foremost
concern as well as her purpose for writing, and since African
people serve as her audience, Morrison, as editor of Chinweizu's
work, must have had more than a passing interest in it. It is one of
the most insightful works that explore the nature of the African's
oppression, expounding the theory that economics precedes
racism. The major premises of the work—that the primary problem confronting Africans is capitalism/imperialism, and that the
solution lies in the unity of African people—would become
major themes in works such as *Tar Baby* and *Beloved*. But even
prior to these works, Toni Morrison uses *Song of Solomon* as
Chinweizu uses *The West and the Rest of Us*, to demonstrate the
important role that African history plays in unearthing the African's primary problem and in unveiling a workable first step in
solving that problem. Thus, the theme of *Song of Solomon* is self-
discovery through knowledge of one's connection to others: one's
family, community, and race.

Several observations made by the renowned African historian
are reflected in Morrison's later works. First and most important
is Chinweizu's position that capitalism gave rise to racism. In
Chapter 19, entitled "Global Power and the Myths of Racism,"
Chinweizu states: "Clearly, both in the genesis of their racism
and in the uses to which they put it, power was fundamental,
racism one of its aides. White power gave birth to white racism,
and white racism serves white power."[9] In *Tar Baby*, Morrison

makes clear her position that capitalism, symbolized by the Valerian Street Candy Company, is the African's primary enemy. Also, like Chinweizu, she takes the time to editorialize on its vicious nature:

> [Valerian] had taken the sugar and cocoa and paid for it as though it had no value, as though the cutting of cane and picking of beans was child's play and had no value; but he turned it into candy, the invention of which was really child's play, and sold it to other children to make a fortune in order to move near, but not in the midst of, the jungle where the sugar came from and build a palace with more of their labor and then hire them to do more of the work he was not capable of and pay them again according to some scale of value that would outrage Satan himself and when those people wanted a little of what he wanted, some apples for *their* Christmas, and took some, he dismissed them with a flutter of the fingers, because they were thieves, and nobody knew thieves and thievery better than he did.[10]

Also clear from this passage is Morrison's understanding that African people are one people, for she makes no distinction between the exploited workers. Therese and Gideon and all the others are referred to as "them."

Chinweizu's second thesis of relevance to this study concerns African solidarity. His belief that solidarity is the only prerequisite to national liberation becomes the prominent thesis of *Beloved*, a novel in which Morrison uses history to show the necessity of collectivism. According to Chinweizu:

> We especially need a solidarity of all who wish to abolish their imperialized condition. But even within that absolute necessary solidarity, let us remember that blacks form a separate constituency.[11]

One other important Chinweizian idea reflected in the Morrison canon is "assimilationist individualism." According to Chinweizu, some African people have been so brainwashed by European propaganda as to believe that all things European are good, all things African are bad. It is a self-hatred that particularly characterizes the African petty bourgeois: "These black universalist individualists seem to believe that by getting away from black solidarity and by applying their talents till their personal achievements shine and dazzle the white man, they will be let in on equal terms into a world elite."[12] What the historian terms assimilationist individualism, we might term *Jadism*, for clearly the female protagonist of *Tar Baby* prefers an inauthentic European self to an authentic African one. Her resistance to all things black—hair, people, nature—is repeatedly examined in the novel.

Rather than a Jadism, African people need a *Sonism*. Chinweizu states: "A socially responsible individualism must be applauded. An individualism that is consciously black oriented, one that recognizes that it must be practiced within the mores of a black African society, for the benefit of Black society and culture . . . and never against the interest of black people."[13]

Toni Morrison gained consciousness not only by reading and editing historical works of Pan-African writers such as Chinweizu, but also by reading literary works. According to the writer and critic Annie Dillard, "The writer studies literature. . . . She is careful of what she reads, for that is what she will write."[14] Certainly, this statement helps us to understand Morrison's practice of borrowing bits and pieces of literary works that have a significant impact on her. This borrowing practice is not unique to Morrison. In African literary history, for example, the act of picking up a word here and a phrase there has been crucial in the development of a collective literary vision. Collectivism is the way in which African people and African literature survive and develop. One of the most profound African literary critics today, Eleanor W. Traylor, astutely refers to this collective process as "commemoration, the art of rememory, a major—but hardly documented—tradition of Afro-American letters."[15] Morrison's commemoration of African works of art succeeds in helping to create a literary continuum. Not merely repeating the past, but extracting the positive and building upon it (in the way that African people must extract the positive from their lives in order to build a wholesome future), Morrison advances the African literary canon and avows her belief in collectivism.

It is important to preface this discussion on Morrison and the art of rememory by the following statement: Morrison's borrowing is conditioned by three important factors. First, the bits and pieces that she picks up are not ideas en masse but choice words, names, or concepts. Second, what she does with these tidbits is usually quite different from and/or more developed than the original author's use of them. And third, the works from which the ideas are borrowed are truly monumental works of art.

Some of the writers from whom it is likely that Morrison borrowed are Ralph Ellison, Alex Haley, Toni Cade Bambara, Henry Dumas, and Middleton Harris.[16] Ellison was perhaps the first major African writer born in the United States who burst the seams of traditional fiction—in context and form. He synthesized myth and reality, folklore and history, in his effort to recreate the world from the perspective of the crisis-ridden African. The protean protagonist of Invisible Man can not only change forms in minuteman fashion in order to create a different reality for himself, but also manipulate visibility. In Ellison's world, Africans can live a life of visibility underground and invisibility above ground! Quite an impressive feat. Morrison was certainly impressed. Ralph Ellison (as well as African writers on the continent), having blazed a trail before her, served as a strong role model. Morrison's characters rise above the harsh conditions of reality in order to recreate themselves. Ultimately, her protagonists develop the ability to heal their schizophrenic personalities and reassert their African selves. In Morrison's world, Africans can be born without navels, fly without wings, and die and be reborn.

As did most Africans familiar with Alex Haley's Roots, Morrison learned the dialectical relationship between discovering one's ancestral roots and discovering one's self. A condensed version of Roots first appeared in Reader's Digest in 1974. It was published two years later in its entirety. On the Acknowledgments page, Haley's last remark is as follows: "The memories of the mouths of the ancient elders was the only way that early histories of mankind got passed along . . . for all of us today to know who we are."[17] Seemingly, this idea of the interconnectedness between past and present impressed Morrison, for it forms the theme of Song of Solomon. Morrison's inscription to Song of Solomon reads: "The fathers may soar, And the children may know their names." Clearly, the underlying premise of both books is that discovering one's roots is a precursor to discovering oneself.

Morrison, however, goes far beyond this basic premise. The plot of Song of Solomon, to take one example, revolves more around the psychological rather than the physical development of the protagonist, a growth from immaturity to maturity based on his knowledge of the past. *Roots*, in contrast, chronicles the generational experiences of one family. Moreover, unlike Haley's work, Morrison has her protagonist acknowledge the role of the nuclear family and the national (racial) community—not just ancestry—in the configuration of his self-identity. Milkman Dead does not become fully conscious of who he is until he has discovered the importance of both male and female members of his family, his community, and his ancestry. Once he does, he soars toward self:

> As fleet and bright as a lodestar he wheeled toward Guitar and it did not matter which one of them would give up his ghost in the killing arms of his brother. For now he knew what Shalimar knew: If you surrendered to the air, you could *ride* it.[18]

Perhaps the most significant morsel that Morrison borrows from Toni Cade Bambara is the concept of the African spirit women who haunt the female protagonist (i.e., Velma Henry) in a conscious-raising effort:

> In the attic they came in the mirror once. Ten or more women with mud hair, strong yams in gourds and pebbles in cracked calabash. And tucking babies in hairy hides. They came like a Polaroid. Stepping out of the mouth of the cave, they tried to climb out of the speckled glass, talk to her, tell her what must be done all over again, all over again, all over again. But she hung an old velvet drape over the mirror and smothered them.[19]

Repeating three times that the struggle for self-identity must be waged over and over again, collectively, not singlehandedly, these mud women try to aid Velma in her search for a wholesome self. Velma, however, smothers them and rejects their advice, and by doing so ensures her own demise.

Evidently, this concept of a haunting collective of African women who come in positive fashion to offer advice to the female protagonist significantly impacted upon Morrison, for she uses it in *Tar Baby*. Jadine, the female protagonist, attempts to escape her identity by becoming the "model" of a European female. Her struggle to escape is repeated again and again in the novel, in her encounter with the woman in yellow, her submersion in the tarlike substance of the Isle des Chevaliers, and, most germane to this discussion, her confrontation with the women "haints" in Eloe. Coming to her in the pitch black Eloe night, these African women shake milk-filled tits at her in their effort to direct her toward her African, woman self:

> "What do you want with me, goddamn it!"
> They looked as though they had just been waiting for that question and they each pulled out a breast and showed it to her. Jadine started to tremble. They stood around in the room, jostling each other gently, gently—there wasn't much room—revealing one breast and then two and Jadine was shocked.[20]

Like Velma, Jadine rejects the sister-women's advice to be what she is—African and woman. Crying out in fear, instead of thanking them, she believes that "the women in the night had killed the whole weekend."[21]

Henry Dumas, as does Toni Morrison, had a deep affection for his people and manifested that affection in his commitment to write about them in ways that he hoped would capture the positive essence of their lives and thereby help them to reclaim the African personality: "I am very much concerned about what is happening to my people and what we are doing with our precious tradition."[22] His collection of writings, like those of Morrison, are not mere factual renditions of African life but art pieces that incorporate surrealism, supernaturalism, astrology, magic, and science fiction.

Morrison first read Dumas's works during the early 1970s. They so impressed her that she helped to organize a book party on his behalf in October 1974. Of him, she writes: "He was thirty-three years old when he was killed, but in those thirty-three years, he had completed work, the quality and quantity of which are almost never achieved in several lifetimes. He was brilliant."[23] From the brilliant works of Dumas, Morrison extracts several key concepts, among them the name "Sweet Home" (the racist Arkansas town in which Dumas was born) and the name "Heyboy" (the dog in one of Dumas's most impressive stories, "Ark of Bones"). Both of these names figure prominently in *Beloved*.

"Ark of Bones" is a surreal, supernatural story about the preservation of the collective consciousness of African people. Through the dedication of the old man of the ark and his helpers, the bones of dead Africans (i.e., the history of African people's struggle to survive in general and their history during the Middle Passage in particular) are fished out, hauled up, and preserved. Heyboy is described as a no-count rabbit dog who, like Here Boy in *Beloved*, mysteriously disappears. The difference between the events surrounding the disappearance of these dogs is that Heyboy's disappearance occurs when the narrator's friend is called to death: "We shook hands and Headeye, he was gone, movin fast with that no-count dog runnin long side him."[24] Here Boy's disappearance occurs when Beloved comes to life: "The rays of the sun struck her [Beloved] full in the face, so that when Sethe, Denver and Paul D rounded the curve in the road all they saw was a black dress, two unlaced shoes below it, and Here Boy nowhere in sight."[25]

As is her habit, Morrison extracts and modifies the Dumas name, Heyboy, as well as the dog's involvement in mysterious circumstances, and tailors them to fit her own set of circumstances. While Dumas's dog is associated with a character who is called to death, death for him is actually life, for he sacrifices his own life to save the lives of future generations of Africans. In Morrison's story, Here Boy is associated with a character who comes to life, but it is a dead life, born of selfish individualism rather than social responsibility.

The contradiction in name and place of Dumas's hometown, Sweet Home, Arkansas, must have greatly impressed the sensitivity of as well as the artist and African in Toni Morrison.[26] The racially segregated Sweet Home was no sweet home for African people living there, especially during Dumas's childhood years; neither is its fictionalized namesake. According to Sethe, physically, the Sweet Home plantation was as beautiful as its name, but for the African, life on it was hell:

And suddenly there was Sweet Home rolling, rolling, rolling out before her eyes, and although there was not a leaf on that farm that did not make her want to scream, it rolled itself out before her in shameless beauty. It never looked as terrible as it was and it made her wonder if hell was a pretty place too. Fire and brimstone all right, but hidden in lacy gloves.[27]

Perhaps the greatest influence on Morrison's writing of *Beloved* was *The Black Book*, a compendium of newsclippings and advertisements chronicling the life of African people in the United States from slavery through the civil rights movement. From this book in general, and in particular the news article entitled "A Visit to the Slave Mother Who Killed Her child," Morrison gets the kernel of her novel: the ex-slave mother so devastated by her own oppression and exploitation in slavery that she murders one of her children to prevent it from experiencing that life; the preacher mother-in-law who witnesses the event and who herself has experienced the oppression and exploitation of giving birth to eight children only to have them stolen from her and sold into slavery; and the slave setting itself, Kentucky, and its adjoining "free" city of Cincinnati, Ohio. Because of its importance in influencing Morrison's consciousness and its relevance to this discussion, most of the news article follows:

I found her with an infant in her arms only a few months old, and observed that it had a large bunch on its forehead. I inquired the cause of the injury. She then proceeded to give a detailed account of her attempt to kill her children.

She said, that when the officers and slave-hunters came to the house in which they were concealed, she caught a shovel and struck two of her children on the head, and then took a knife and cut the throat of the third, and tried to kill the other,—that if they had given her time, she would have killed them all—that with regard to herself, she cared but little, but she was unwilling to have her children suffer as she had done.

I inquired if she was not excited almost to madness when she committed the act. No, she replied, I was as cool as I am now; and would much rather kill them at once, and thus end their sufferings, than have them taken back to slavery, and be murdered by piece-meal. She then told the story of her wrongs. She spoke of her days of suffering, of her nights of unmitigated toil, while the bitter tears coursed their way down her cheeks and fell in the face of the innocent child as it looked smiling up, little conscious of the danger and probable suffering that awaited it. . . .

The two men and the two other children were in another apartment, but her mother-in-law was in the same room. She says she is the mother of eight children, most of whom have been separated from her; that her husband was once separated from her twenty-five years, during which time she did not see him; that could she have prevented it, she would never have permitted him to return, as she did not wish him to witness her sufferings, or be exposed to the brutal treatment that he would receive.

She states that she has been a faithful servant, and in her old age she would not have attempted to obtain her liberty; but as she became feeble, and less capable of performing labor, her master became more and more exacting and brutal in his treatment, until she could stand it no longer; that the effort could result only in death, at most—she therefore made the attempt.

She witnessed the killing of the child, but said she neither encouraged nor discouraged her daughter-in-law,—for under similar circumstances she should probably have done the same. The old woman is from sixty to seventy years of age, has been a professor of religion about twenty years, and speaks with much feeling of the time when she shall be delivered from the power of the oppressor, and dwell with the Savior, "where the wicked cease from troubling, and the weary are at rest."

These slaves (as far as I am informed) have resided all their lives within sixteen miles of Cincinnati. We are frequently told that Kentucky slavery is very innocent. If these are its fruits, where it exists in a mild form, will some one tell us what we may expect from its more objectionable features? But comments are unnecessary.   P.S. Bassett.
  Fairmount Theological Seminary,
  Cincinnati, (Ohio,) Feb. 12, 1856.

With the essence of this newsclip, Morrison concocts the *Beloved* story.[28] What she does with this story, however, is to expand, refine, and shape it so that *Beloved* picks up where *Tar Baby* leaves off. Evidently, what clicked in her mind—perhaps not at first, but later while mulling over this news article—was the fact that conditions then and now as well as our reactions to them have not qualitatively changed. Revealing in *Tar Baby* that capitalism in all its forms, including slavery, is the primary cause of the African's oppression and exploitation, Morrison uses *Beloved* to pose the solution which can best begin to address this crisis: collective struggle. *Beloved's* haunting presence at 124 Bluestone Road is a warning to Sethe and to the entire African world that even the death of one African jeopardizes the well-being of the collective. Hi Man voices Morrison's own philosophy: "One lost,

all lost. The chain that held them would save all or none."[29]
"Sixty Million and more" lost in slavery is enough. At least
Morrison thinks so because it is with this phrase that she in-
scribes *Beloved*.

One of the most conclusive pieces of evidence demonstrating
Toni Morrison's habit of borrowing kernels of ideas from historical and literary works is her practice of borrowing from herself.
Evidently, writing is discovery for her, for early ideas show up,
greatly expanded, in later works. The writing process itself, then,
is another factor to be considered in understanding the author's
developing class consciousness.

The very fact that her works are developmental suggests that
Morrison discovers more about herself, her people, and her society as a consequence of the writing process. She herself substantiates this fact in an interview with Claudia Tate: "Writing is
discovery; it's talking deep within myself, 'deep talking' as you
say."[30] This deep talking allows Morrison to examine more
closely ideas already promulgated in her works as well as to
discover new ones in the work she is composing. That is, not
only is she discovering self at the moment of writing, but also
afterwards, during the incubation period between completing
one novel and beginning another. For example, embryo ideas and
characters that appear in early works appear more fully developed and/or play a more dominant role in later ones: milk as
nurturing substance, the one or defected leg motif, Virginia as
setting, the golden-eyed males, the flight motif, the three women,
and so on. Jane Bakerman acknowledges the existence of this
inbetween incubation period. However, while she offers several
valid reasons for its existence, she overlooks that which is primary—Morrison's own self-discovery:

> Generally, it takes Morrison about two to two and a half years to
> produce a novel, and there are several reasons for that time span. One
> is that she aims for a genuinely polished beautiful whole. . . . An-
> other reason for the substantial incubation times for the novels is the
> simple fact that Toni Morrison is a very busy person, busy being
> mother, editor, and teacher, as well as author.[31]

Most crucial in understanding this time span is Morrison's own
need to think about the new ideas that have surfaced during the
writing process. And by taking time to read and to think, she

grows more and more conscious of her thematic and structural creations. In short, she becomes increasingly aware of the problems confronting African people (the substance) and the best solution for addressing them (the form). She herself corroborates the fact that the developmental stages experienced by her are in part contributed to by the act of writing:

> After my first novel, The Bluest Eye, writing became a way to be coherent in the world. It became necessary and possible for me to sort out the past, and the selection process, being disciplined and guided, was genuine thinking. . . . Writing gives me what I think dancers have on stage in relation to gravity and space and time. It is energetic and balanced, fluid and in repose. And there is always the possibility of growth.[32]

Moreover, because writing is discovery, Morrison admits to choosing topics to which she does not know the answers: "It's out of what I don't know that I begin to write, not what I know. If I know it, I probably wouldn't write about it because there is not discovery."[33]

Finally, this study would be incomplete if nothing were said about the limits of Toni Morrison's consciousness, if, in fact, the implication of this study was that with the writing of Beloved, Morrison demonstrates full consciousness of the nation-class oppression of African people and the complex solution that will eliminate this oppression. One comment Morrison makes that justifies such a discussion as this is that "if there were better criticism, there would be better books."[34] Hopefully, this assessment of her consciousness will aid her in positing a more concrete, viable plan for the national liberation of African people.

With the writing of Beloved, Morrison provides African people with many of the ingredients necessary for waging a successful struggle against oppression. She has identified the primary cause of this oppression: capitalism in all of its disguises (Tar Baby). She has explored the effects of this cause: racism and sexism (Song of Solomon). She has unmasked the awful devastation caused by both the cause and the effects (The Bluest Eye, Sula, and Beloved). She has proven that the strategies of political education (i.e., communicating the word) and African unification are essential in the struggle (Tar Baby and Beloved). However, while Morrison makes clear what African people are struggling against and while she makes clear the strategy that equips them for this struggle—solidarity, she never makes clear what African people are struggling *for*. That is, the question of what type of lifestyle is needed for us to revitalize the African personality is left unaddressed in the Morrison canon. In this respect, one of the primary weaknesses existing in the world of *Beloved* is that while collectivism exists at 124 Bluestone when Sethe and Denver arrive, the enemy (in this case, the slavemaster) can at any time, and does, shatter it.

Thus, Morrison's canon does not demonstrate the author's full consciousness of the relation of land, and the development of it, to African people's wholesome existence. Unlike Marcus Garvey, Malcolm X, Shirley Graham DuBois, and Kwame Nkrumah, Morrison has not yet demonstrated a clear understanding of the fact that until Africa is free and united, no African worldwide will ever be free.

Three essential ingredients necessary for the survival of the nation are omitted from Toni Morrison's world view: the necessity for a land base, the need for international African solidarity in recognition of Africans as one people with a common struggle against a common enemy, and the necessity for planned development (i.e., scientific socialism) for the benefit of all African people, not just a handful of Africans.

In *Beloved*, the insular, ex-slave community of Cincinnati reflects a type of land base operating for the benefit of all those within it. However, this type of existence is problematic. First, the land rightfully belongs to the Native American Indian, not the African (the only land that rightfully belongs to the person of African descent is Africa). Second, it is land that is easily penetrable by the enemy. Thus, instead of determining and planning for his or her destiny, the African is at the mercy of those who dominate the land, the European. Only a liberated, unified Africa would ensure a viable future, a power base from which the African can demand human justice, no matter where he or she decides to reside in the world. According to W. E. B. DuBois, "Until Africa is free, the descendants of Africa the world over cannot escape chains."[35] Marcus Garvey advised Africans everywhere to "build up in Africa a government of our own, big enough and strong enough to protect Africa and Negroes everywhere."[36] Even Malcolm was clear on the question of "Africa for

Africans, those at home and those abroad." According to him, "The only hope for the black man in America [is] in a strong Africa."[37] It is with the words of Kwame Nkrumah, however, that the land question receives its clearest articulation:

> The core of the Black Revolution is in Africa, and until Africa is united under a socialist government, the Black man throughout the world lacks a national home. It is around the African peoples' struggle for liberation and unification that African or Black culture will take shape and substance. Africa is one continent, one people, and one nation.[38]

In choosing the Caribbean as the setting for *Tar Baby*, Toni Morrison comes closest to articulating the common identity of African people and the common oppression experienced by them. Clearly, she understands that international capitalism affects Gideon and Therese as it does Sydney and Ondine. As Stokely Carmichael (now Kwame Ture) states, the only significant difference between the African in the diaspora and Africans at home is that "one group was taken from the land (slavery), the second group had the land taken from them (colonialism)."[39] Certainly, Africans have more in common with themselves than with any other nationality. As Garvey stated, there is "absolutely no difference between the native African and the American and West Indian Negroes in that we are descendants from one family stock."[40]

Finally, while Morrison is quite clear on the vicious nature of capitalism as demonstrated in *Tar Baby* and *Beloved*, and while she shows her reader the positive rewards of collective work and responsibility in all of her works, especially *Beloved*, she never explicitly states that planned development of the economy is a prerequisite for the survival and advancement of African people. Just as Africans have a common heritage and culture, so do they have a common struggle against capitalism/imperialism and a common struggle for socialism: "Until there is an All-African Union Government pursuing socialist policies, and planning the economic development of Africa as a whole, the standard of living of the African masses will remain low, and they will continue to suffer."[41] Nowhere does she demonstrate an awareness of the principles of scientific socialism: production for use, not profit; planned methods of production; political power in the hands of the people; and the application of scientific methods in all spheres of thought and production.

Without a free and united homeland, without a unification of African people throughout the world, without scientific socialism, African people will continue to wage a constant but ineffective struggle against their nation-class oppression. Hopefully, Toni Morrison will come to understand, embrace, and advocate Pan-Africanism: the total liberation and unification of Africa under scientific socialism.

Notes

Chapter 1. Nkrumaism and the Novels of Toni Morrison

1. Emile Burns, *An Introduction to Marxism* (New York: International Publishers, 1966), 18.
2. Thiong'O Wa Ngugi, *Homecoming: Essays on African and Caribbean Literature, Culture and Politics* (New York: Lawrence Hill and Company, 1972), xv.
3. Burns, *An Introduction to Marxism*, 21.
4. Ibid., 101.
5. Walter Rodney, *How Europe Underdeveloped Africa* (Dar es Salaam: Tanzania Publishing House, 1972), 13.
6. Burns, *An Introduction to Marxism*, 54.
7. Samora Machel, "Establishing People's Power to Serve the Masses," in *Samora Machel: An African Revolutionary*, ed. Barry Munslow (London: Zed Books, Ltd., 1985), 4.
8. Rodney, *How Europe Underdeveloped Africa*, 18.
9. Ibid., 99–100.
10. *Webster's Third New International Dictionary of the English Language*, Unabridged (Springfield, Mass.: G. & C. Merriam Company, 1976).
11. Rodney, *How Europe Underdeveloped Africa*, 99–100.
12. Kwame Nkrumah, *Class Struggle in Africa* (New York: International Publishers, 1970), 29.
13. Eric Williams, *Capitalism and Slavery* (New York: G. P. Putnam's Sons, 1944), 18–19.
14. Ibid., 7–8.
15. Rodney, *How Europe Underdeveloped Africa*, 100.
16. Nkrumah, *Class Struggle in Africa*, 27.
17. A condensed version of *Roots* was serialized in the *Reader's Digest* in 1974; the entire work was first published in 1976.
18. Toni Morrison, *Song of Solomon* (New York: New American Library, 1977), 336.
19. Judith Wilson, "A Conversation with Toni Morrison," *Essence* 12 (July 1981): 86.
20. Susan Willis, "Eruptions of Funk: Historicizing Toni Morrison," in *Black Literature and Literary Theory*, ed. Henry Louis Gates, Jr. (New York: Methuen, 1984), 270.
21. Ibid., 268.
22. Toni Morrison says that she writes for an African audience in particular. In an interview with Claudia Tate, she remarked: "When I view the world, perceive it and write about it, it's the world of Black people." Claudia Tate, ed., *Black Women Writers at Work* (New York: Continuum, 1985), 118. On another occasion, she stated: "I use myself as the Black audience." Jane Bakerman,

" 'The Seams Can't Show': An Interview with Toni Morrison," *Black American Literature Forum* 12, no. 2 (Summer 1978): 59.

23. Kwame Nkrumah, *Consciencism: Philosophy and Ideology for De-Colonization* (New York: Modern Reader, 1964), 69.

24. Barbara Christian, "Community and Nature: The Novels of Toni Morrison," *The Journal of Ethnic Studies* 7 (1980): 4, 65.

25. Robert E. Stepto, " 'Intimate Things in Place': A Conversation with Toni Morrison," in *Chant of Saints*, ed. Michael S. Harper and Robert E. Stepto (Urbana: University of Illinois Press, 1979), 214. For additional discussions on traditional African principles reflected in Morrison's works, see Peter B. Erickson's article, "Images of Nurturance in Toni Morrison's *Tar Baby*," *CLA Journal* 28, no. 1 (September 1984): 20. See also Bettye J. Parker, "Complexity: Toni Morrison's Women—An Interview Essay," in *Sturdy Black Bridges*, ed. Roseann Bell, Bettye J. Parker, and Beverly Guy-Sheftall (New York: Anchor Press, 1979).

26. Christian, "Community and Nature," 78.

27. Barbara Christian, *Black Feminist Criticism* (New York: Pergamon Press, 1985), 65.

28. Jacqueline DeWeever, "The Inverted World of Toni Morrison's *The Bluest Eye* and *Sula*," *CLA Journal* 22, no. 4 (June 1979): 408.

29. Grace Ann Hovet and Barbara Lounsberry, "Flying as Symbol and Legend in Toni Morrison's *The Bluest Eye, Sula,* and *Song of Solomon, CLA Journal* 27, no. 2 (December 1983): 121.

30. Julie J. Nichols, "Patterns in Toni Morrison's Novels," *English Journal* 72 (January 1983): 46.

31. Ibid., 47–48.

32. Wilson, "Conversations," 134; Tate, ed., *Black Women Writers at Work,* 119.

33. S. G. Ikoku, "Aspects of Consciencism," *Pan-African Review* 1, no. 2 (1964): 101.

Chapter 2. The *Bluest Eye:* The Need for Racial Approbation

1. Toni Morrison, *The Bluest Eye* (New York: Washington Square Press, 1970), 24.

2. Toni Morrison's decision to use an African female as protagonist reflects her interest in gender oppression as well as race and class oppression. In fact, all three forms of oppression are explored in each of Morrison's works. However, their primacy varies depending on the author's level of consciousness. In *The Bluest Eye*, sexism, like class exploitation, plays a secondary role to race oppression. Morrison does make clear, however, that the African female is the most vulnerable to capitalist propaganda in the United States, for it is the female in general who, in the United States, has often had her worth measured in terms of beauty rather than character or accomplishment. Also, Morrison's concern with gender oppression is reflected in the rape of Pecola. Pecola's rape and subsequent pregnancy further isolate her from society and, therefore, hasten her flight into insanity.

3. Morrison, *The Bluest Eye,* 34.

4. The Harlem Renaissance poet and novelist, Jean Toomer, made clear this

association between the European female's hair and lynching in his short poem, "Portrait in Georgia":

Hair—braided chesnut, coiled like a lyncher's rope.
Eyes—fagots
Lips—old scars, or the first red blisters,
Breath—the last sweet scent of cane
And her slim body, white as the ash of black flesh after
    flame.

Toni Morrison, student of African literature and former English major and teacher, is certainly aware of Toomer's poem. Her point that Maureen Peal's hair resembles lynch ropes is intended to remind the reader of this poem and thus to elicit feelings of apprehension and ugliness rather than beauty.

5. Morrison, The Bluest Eye, 53.
6. Ibid., 57.
7. Ibid., 61.
8. Keith E. Byerman's comment on the skin-color conflict in The Bluest Eye reflects the extent of Morrison's emphasis on race: "Morrison describes a social situation so distorted by the myth of whiteness that it produces a child, Pecola, who is so obsessed by the blue-eyed beauty of Shirley Temple that she creates a self-contained reality that cannot be penetrated even by rape and incest." "Intense Behaviors: The Use of the Grotesque in The Bluest Eye and Eva's Man," CLA Journal 25 (June 1982): 448. Also Chikwenye Ogunyemi's insightful statement on the significance of the novel's title emphasizes the issue of race as Morrison's thematic concern: "The bluest eye can be a pun on 'the bluest I,' the gloomy ego, the black man feeling very blue from the psychological bombardment he is exposed to from early life to late. The novel is, then, a blues enunciating the pain of the black man in America and an attempt to grapple with the pain which is sometimes existential. The superlative 'bluest' implies that the other groups are 'blue' and 'bluer'—and, of course, the black race is the 'bluest.' " "Order and Disorder in Toni Morrison's The Bluest Eye," Critique 19, no. 1 (1977): 114.
9. Morrison, The Bluest Eye, 71.
10. Ibid., 132.
11. Ibid., 133.
12. Ibid., 133.
13. According to Barbara Christian, "Morrison's use of the inversion of the truth is sifted. So that the seasonal flow of birth, death and rebirth is inverted in the human society." Christian, "Community and Nature," 74.
14. The structural problems of the text have led some critics such as Jacqueline DeWeever to believe that there is only one narrator. According to DeWeever, "Claudia tells the story from her point of view, presenting the world of three little black girls. DeWeever, "The Inverted World," 404.
15. Morrison, The Bluest Eye, 62.
16. Phyllis R. Klotman, "Dick-and-Jane and the Shirley Temple Sensibility in The Bluest Eye," Black American Literature Forum 13, no. 4 (Winter 1979): 123–24.
17. Bakerman, " 'The Seams Can't Show,' " 59.
18. Stepto, " 'Intimate Things in Place,' " 222.
19. Morrison, The Bluest Eye, 7.

Chapter 3. Sula: The Struggle for Individual Fulfillment

1. Karen F. Stein, "Toni Morrison's Sula: A Black Woman's Epic," Black American Literature Forum (Winter 1984): 149.
2. Toni Morrison, Sula (New York: New American Library, 1973), 52.
3. Ibid., 92.
4. See Alice Walker's The Temple of My Familiar for a more realistic presentation of the options available to women. According to Walker, women since the beginning of their existence have been creative—despite their oppressive conditions. In fact, Walker shows that women have been creative in creating these options, even in regard to art.
5. Bakerman, " 'The Seams Can't Show,' " 60.
6. Morrison, Sula, 51.
7. Ibid., 52.
8. Parker, "Complexity," 253.
9. Morrison, Sula, 53.
10. Ibid., 168.
11. Ibid., 95.
12. Ibid., 83.
13. Ibid., 149.
14. Ibid., 92.
15. While Barbara Christian restricts her analysis of the individual's quest for self-fulfillment outside of the fulfillment of the community to women only, she nevertheless accurately characterizes the negative consequences of such a search: "[Sula] seeks her own individuality as a means to self-fulfillment. But as a woman, her desire to make herself rather than others goes against the most basic principle of the community's struggle to survive." Christian, "Community and Nature," 70.
16. In his commitment to struggle for a wholesome life for himself and the rest of the Bottom community, and in his recognition of himself as an African (Shadrack looks into the blackness of the toilet and gains comfort), Shadrack is a forerunner of Son. See Byerman's comment for a different view. "[Shadrack] is deprived of all the markers of an identity." Keith E. Byerman, Fingering the Jagged Grain: Tradition and Form in Recent Black Fiction (Athens: The University of Georgia Press, 1985), 194.
17. Morrison, Sula, 119.
18. Ibid., 122.
19. Ibid., 145. Critics such as Cynthia Davis and Karen Stein, who celebrate in Morrison's development of a protagonist who indulges in self, read her canon as a static rather than a dynamic body of literature. According to Davis, Morrison characters such as Sula "are clearly existential heroes, 'free' in the Sartrean sense of being their own creators." Cynthia Davis, "Self, Society, and Myth in Toni Morrison's Fiction," Contemporary Literature 23, no. 3 (Summer 1982): 331. Stein writes that "the ability to survive in the face of a hostile world and to accept one's fate in full self-knowledge constitutes the real nobility left to the heroes." Stein, "Toni Morrison's Sula," 149. Moreover, both critics fail to see the contradictions that exist in the work itself: that Morrison, on the one hand, points to the societal limitations of the female as the culprit, and on the other hand, blames the individual's severing of communal ties. Clearly, the events surrounding National Suicide Day (1941) negate the notion that either mere survival of a community or individual existence outside of the community is viable for African people.

20. Morrison, *Sula*, 117.
21. Ibid., 112.
22. Ibid., 96.
23. Ibid., 117–18.
24. Ibid., 114.
25. Ibid., 115.
26. It seems a reflection of Morrison's immature consciousness that she has the Bottom community band together and act positively as a result of perceived evil in the community. Usually, positive action brings positive results; negative action creates negative results. Perhaps unconsciously Morrison understands this dialectic because the unity created in the Bottom as a result of Sula's negative, self-centered behavior is short-lived, artificial unity. Morrison will come to fully understand that the positive actions of a Son and a Paul D will spark a higher level of consciousness among the people in the community.
27. Christian, "Community and Nature," 67.
28. Morrison, *Sula*, 149.
29. Ibid., 5.
30. Ibid., 133.
31. Ibid., 160.
32. Ibid., 161–62.
33. Ibid., 90.
34. Christian, "Community and Nature," 71.
35. Stein, "Toni Morrison's *Sula*," 149.
36. It is important to distinguish between Nel the twelve-year-old girl and Nel the woman. Unlike Sula's, Nel's consciousness of herself in relationship to the community grows. As a child, Nel is more of a free spirit like Sula. Her free-spiritedness is reflected in her complicity with Sula in the death of Chicken Little. As a woman, however, Nel recognizes the importance of the community in the development of the individual, a mature recognition that brings with it social responsibility (e.g., visiting the nursing home where Eva lives) and that moves her closer to the thinking and behavior of the adult community (and further from the thinking and behavior of Sula). See also Stepto's interview with Morrison in which Morrison reveals that Nel is the community since "she believes in its values." Stepto, " 'Intimate Things in Place,' " 216.
37. Morrison, *Sula*, 163.
38. Ibid., 165.
39. Ibid., 20–21.
40. Ibid., 23.
41. Ibid., 24.
42. Ibid., 174.
43. Barbara Christian's insightful comment on Morrison's recognition of the fruitlessness of the individual pursuit for freedom is relevant in pointing up Morrison's own ambivalence in regard to the idea that individual fulfillment outside the community is the answer for African women: "Morrison resists the idea that either individual pursuit or community conservatism is enough for fulfillment. Left without a context, the self has 'no speck from which to grow,' and deprived of creative spirits the community succumbs to death and destruction." "Community and Nature," 71. Morrison's failure to fully recognize this dialectic operating between the individual and the community is reflected in the solution she proposes in *Sula*.
44. Morrison, *Sula*, 121.

45. Sekou Toure, "Africa on Walk: Revolution and Religion," International Ideological Symposium, Conakry, Guinea, November 13–16, 1978.

46. Morrison, *Sula*, 51.

47. Barbara Lounsberry and Grace Hovet, "Principles of Perception in Toni Morrison's *Sula*, *Black American Literature Forum* 13, no. 4 (Winter 1979): 128.

48. Indirectly, however, the Chicken Little episode lends further credence to Morrison's point that racism is alive and flourishing in the United States. The European who finds Chicken Little's body "shook his head in disgust at the kind of parents who would drown their own children. When, he wondered, will those people ever be anything but animals, fit for nothing but substitutes for mules, only mules didn't kill each other the way niggers did." Morrison, *Sula*, 63.

Chapter 4. *Song of Solomon:* The Struggle for Race and Class Consciousness

1. Chinweizu, *The West and the Rest of Us: White Predators, Black Slaves and the African Elite* (New York: Random House, 1975), 232.

2. In an interview with Robert Stepto, Morrison makes a statement that indicates that she, herself, sees her work as a developing canon: "And his [Macon Dead, Jr.'s] son is the main character who makes friends with people in the community that is described in *Sula*. Stepto, " 'Intimate Things in Place,' " 222. It is interesting to note in this connection that Sula dies at thirty and Milkman develops consciousness at thirty-one.

3. As editor for Random House, Morrison edited the works of conscious Africans like Chinweizu. He pays tribute to her in his acknowledgments page. Morrison seems to have been particularly influenced by this work because some of the ideas present in *Song of Solomon* are quite similar to ones advanced by Chinweizu, especially those on African identity. See Chinweizu, *The West and the Rest of Us*, 224–26.

4. In regard to theme, Richard K. Barksdale astutely writes that Morrison "turns upside down many of the established social, moral and cultural beliefs that the Western world has inherited from the Judeo-Christian and Greco-Roman traditions." Richard K. Barksdale, "*Song of Solomon*," *World Literature Today* 52 (Summer 1978): 465. In regard to structure, see Barbara Harris's comments in "Myth as Structure in Toni Morrison's *Song of Solomon*, *Melus* 7, no. 3 (Fall 1980): 71. Harris describes the sophisticated narrative form of *Song of Solomon*:

> The textual richness of the novel derives from a present which spans three generations, with each narrative tied back into the development of the novel's hero. The digressions, explanations, and expansions which interrupt Milkman's own story suggest not a serial or chronological unfolding but an interlace, in which dominant narrative is embellished and enhanced through meticulously articulated subplots and images threading their way through Milkman's life (P. 71).

5. The terms used to describe each of Milkman's developmental stages are adapted from those of the anthropologist Arnold van Gennep, found in his

chapter "The Territorial Passage" in the work *Rites of Passage.* I do not attempt to apply Gennep's definitions of the territorial stages verbatim; nor do I, always, use the stages within the same context. Rather, I extract the terminology and tailor it to fit my analysis (for an alternative classification system, see Dorothy Lee's "To Ride the Air," in which she divides Milkman's development into four stages: initiation, renunciation, atonement, and release [P. 64]).

While each of the three developmental stages has its own distinguishable characteristics, there is overlapping present. As dialectics tell us, there is positive and negative (contradictions) in everything and everyone; however, one is always dominant. Thus, while Milkman exhibits characteristics that are predominantly negative in his preliminary stage, there are positive characteristics present as well. They are just overshadowed by the negative.

6. Toni Morrison, *Song of Solomon* (New York: New American Library, 1977), 68.

7. Ibid., 75.

8. Ibid., 90–91.

9. According to Joyce M. Wegs, "Milkman's repeated urination in inappropriate contexts symbolizes his self-concern, his indifference to others, and his childishness." Joyce M. Wegs, "Toni Morison's *Song of Solomon:* A Blues Song," *Essays in Literature* 9, no. 2 (Fall 1982): 218.

10. Morrison, *Song of Solomon,* 47.

11. Ibid., 37.

12. In fact, the women of the novel become the gauge by which to measure Milkman's maturing race and class consciousness. For example, Pilate's role in the novel is dialectically related to Milkman's developing consciousness. When Milkman first sees her, she is sitting with one foot pointing east and one west. Because east points to Africa and its culture and, thus, to Milkman's past, and west points to the Western world and its culture and, thus, to Milkman's present and future, Pilate symbolizes the bridge that connects the two. She is the source, the base from which Milkman must build his race and class consciousness.

13. Morrison, *Song of Solomon,* 282.

14. Ibid., 81.

15. Ibid., 68.

16. Ibid., 70.

17. Ibid., 69–70.

18. Ibid., 62.

19. Ibid., 35.

20. Ibid., 78.

21. Ibid., 88.

22. Barbara Christian writes that Macon Dead, Sr.'s philosophy is shared by the rising African middle class. "Community and Nature," 71.

23. Morrison, *Song of Solomon,* 150.

24. Ibid., 106.

25. Ibid., 79.

26. Ibid., 120.

27. Ibid., 113.

28. Ibid., 126.

29. Ibid., 161.

30. Ibid., 122.

31. Ibid., 154.

32. Ibid., 156.
33. Ibid., 157.
34. Ibid., 161.
35. Ibid., 210–11.
36. Ibid., 211.
37. Ibid., 211.
38. Ibid., 179. It is interesting to note that Milkman drives into Shalimar in a Buick, connecting his low level of class consciousness here with that which he possesses in the peacock scene.
39. Morrison, *Song of Solomon*, 180.
40. Ibid., 281.
41. Ibid., 274.
42. Ibid., 280.
43. Ibid., 284.
44. Ibid., 278. In the Morrisonian canon, psychological growth is measured both by physiological changes and physical distance. Milkman's journey first to Danville, then to Shalimar, portends his heightened consciousness.
45. Morrison, *Song of Solomon*, 234.
46. Ibid., 282.
47. Morrison's class analysis was sharpened by editing *The West*. In that work, Chinweizu discusses class suicide:

> The African decolonization movement was organized, dominated and guided by, and for the benefit of, that 1 percent of Africans who sought to make gains within colonial society by mobilizing the people and agitating in the name of the whole nation. Their leaders, like leaders everywhere, had to serve the interest of their class if they were to remain leaders. Where their class interest coincided with the people's interest they served both simultaneously; where these interests diverged they always served their class but systematically contrived to appear to be serving the nation as a whole. What was good for their class they saw as good for the whole nation. Their class was their true nation. Given their position and ambition, radical militancy on their part would have mounted to self-betrayal, and perhaps class suicide (P. 146).

After writing and digesting the contents of *Song of Solomon*, Morrison's analysis will sharpen even more. In both *Song of Solomon* and *Tar Baby*, Morrison uses the color silver to symbolize the wealth and status of the ruling class as well as the petty bourgeois aspirations of Africans. See Bonnie S. Lange for an alternative point of view. According to her, "Milkman's silver-backed brushes are a symbol of betrayal." Bonnie S. Lange, "Toni Morrison's Rainbow Code," *Critique* 24 (Spring 1983): 179.
48. Morrison, *Song of Solomon*, 269.
49. Ibid., 268.
50. Ibid., 281–82.
51. Ibid., 339.
52. Ibid., 319.
53. Ibid., 186.
54. Ibid., 122.
55. Ibid., 123.
56. Ibid., 280.
57. Ibid., 288–89.

58. Barksdale, "Song of Solomon," 465.
59. Morrison, Song of Solomon, 340.
60. Ibid., 288–89.
61. Ibid., 5.
62. Ibid., 152.
63. Ibid., 153.
64. Ibid., 130.
65. Cynthia Davis has a different interpretation of Morrison's use of a male protagonist. According to this critic, Morrison "is quite able to show black women as victims, as understanding narrators, or even as 'free' in the sense of disconnection. But when the time comes to fulfill the myth, to show a hero who goes beyond the independence to engagement, she creates a male hero. Her own emphasis on the effect of particulars on meaning raises questions about that choice." "Self, Society, and Myth," 337.
66. Nkrumah, Class Struggle in Africa, 27.
67. Morrison, Song of Solomon, 341.
68. See Grace Ann Hovet's comment on Milkman's potential to engage in conscious action: "At the end of Song of Solomon, she [Morrison] describes her main character, Milkman Dead, as a fleet and bright 'lodestar,' indicating thereby his ability to lead." Hovet and Lounsberry, "Flying," 140.
69. Nkrumah, Consciencism, 78.
70. While Dorothy H. Lee astutely acknowledges the expansion of consciousness achieved by the union of Milkman and Guitar, she sees this union in, of, and by itself as liberating. Like other critics, she views the discovery of self as the end all. Dorothy H. Lee, "Song of Solomon: To Ride the Air," Black American Literature Forum 16, no. 2 (Summer 1982): 64–70. For similar views, see also Leslie A. Harris, "Myth as Structure in Toni Morrison's Song of Solomon," Multi-Ethnic Literature of the U.S. 7, no. 3 (Fall 1980): 75 and Davis, "Self, Society, and Myth," 336. Grace Ann Hovet and Barbara Lounsberry offer a refreshingly different and expanded view of Milkman's goal: "Milkman gains his identity at the end of the novel when he understands his relationship to the past and develops imaginative and responsible love for those in his present. How he can transmit his insights and love, now gained, is only hinted at in the conclusion of Song of Solomon. Like Milkman, we are left in midair at the end of the novel. But also like him, we have learned 'what it takes to fly.' " "Flying," 140. Additionally, Virginia Hamilton's version of the flying African myth serves as another important way of judging the ending of Song of Solomon and assessing Morrison's level of consciousness at this point in her writing career. According to the myth, the African with the knowledge of flight used his awareness to help other Africans to fly: "[Toby] cried out to the fallen and reached his arms out to them. 'Kum kunka yali, kum . . . tambe!' Whispers and sighs. And they too rose on the air." Virginia Hamilton, The People Could Fly: American Black Folktales (New York: Alfred A. Knopf, 1985), p. 170.

Chapter 5. Tar Baby: A Reflection of Morrison's Developed Class Consciousness

1. In discussing the ending of Tar Baby with Judith Wilson, Morrison states: "The problem has been put in the wrong place, as though it's a sexual battle, not

a cultural one. Racism hurts in a very personal way. Because of it, people do all sorts of things in their personal lives and love relationships based on differences in values and class and education and their conception of what it means to be Black in this society." Wilson, "Conversation," 133. This statement suggests that Morrison, after writing *Tar Baby*, understands the triple plight of African people. It also suggests that she is still unclear about the dominant role of class, although such a clarity is quite evident in the work itself. Perhaps the author had not yet fully digested the information presented in the novel.

2. Nkrumah, *Class Struggle in Africa*, 87.

3. Toni Morrison, *Tar Baby* (New York: New American Library, 1981), 132.

4. It is another example of Morrison's heightened consciousness that she chooses two protagonists for this novel—one male and the other female.

5. For additional information on the terms *people capitalism, enlightened capitalism, class peace,* and *class harmony,* see Nkrumah's *Class Struggle in Africa,* 87.

6. The terms *humanism, collectivism,* and *egalitarianism* are defined in chapter 1 of this book.

7. Eric Williams, in chapter 1 of *Capitalism and Slavery,* his economic study on the role of African slavery and the slave trade in providing the capital that financed the Industrial Revolution, writes: "Negro slavery, thus, had nothing to do with climate. Its origin can be expressed in three words: in the Caribbean, Sugar; on the mainland, Tobacco and Cotton" (p. 23).

8. Morrison, *Tar Baby*, 174.

9. On numerous occasions, Morrison has stated that she writes for an African audience. See note 4 in chap. 1 for citations.

10. Morrison, *Tar Baby*, 124.

11. Ibid., 178.

12. Ibid., 46.

13. Ibid., 51.

14. Ibid., 137, 82.

15. Ibid., 32, 87.

16. Ibid., 140.

17. According to Morrison, "In the original story, the tar baby is made by a white man—that has to be the case with Jadine. She has to have been almost 'constructed' by the Western thing, and grateful to it." See Wilson, "Conversation," 130.

18. Morrison, *Tar Baby*, 77.

19. Ibid., 77.

20. Ibid., 103.

21. Ibid., 101.

22. Ibid., 175.

23. Ibid., 57.

24. Ibid., 61–62.

25. Ibid., 38.

26. Keith E. Byerman perceptively writes that Jadine "chooses the fixed life of white values, which are repeatedly associated with death, to the uncertainties of her race, which Morrison consistently associates with life and nature. Moreover, she chooses in effect to be a creation rather than a creator, an art historian rather than artist." Byerman, *Fingering the Jagged Grain*, 213.

27. Morrison, *Tar Baby*, 39.

28. Ibid., 133–34.

29. Ibid., 155.
30. Ibid., 154.
31. Ibid., 54.
32. Ibid., 156.
33. Ibid., 241, 242.
34. Ibid., 81.
35. Ibid., 1.
36. Ibid., 149.
37. Ibid., 97.
38. Ibid., 135.
39. Ibid., 124.
40. Ibid., 120.
41. Son's dizzy, faint feeling after hearing the story of the race of African blind people may also result from the recognition of his relationship to it. Son's association with this race on the Isle des Chevaliers is made from the beginning. Refer to pages 86, 90, 91, and 130 of *Tar Baby* for relevant passages.
42. Morrison, *Tar Baby*, 258.
43. Ibid., 196. It is interesting that Morrison names this African sister Nommo. Keith Byerman reveals that "in Africa, *nommo* (the word) creates reality." Byerman, *Fingering the Jagged Grain*, 6. However, Jadine is not at all changed by her meeting of Nommo. Nommo's experiences as both an African and a female do not bring home to Jadine the reality of the majority of African people in the United States.
44. Dreams have always played a significant role in Morrison's canon, particularly in reflecting the protagonists' level of consciousness in regard to African people. In *Song of Solomon*, Milkman—during his unconscious stage—dreams of his mother's aphixiation by plants as he idly stands by and watches. In *Tar Baby*, Son dreams of "yellow houses with white doors which women opened and shouted Come on in, you honey you! and the fat black ladies in white dresses minding the pie table in the basement of the church and the white wet sheets flapping on a line, and the sound of a six-string guitar plucked after supper while children scooped walnuts up off the ground" (p. 102). That Son has these dreams reveals his sensitivity to and love for African people and the African way of life. However, that he tries to insert these dreams into Jadine as a way of politically educating her reveals his idealism, his fairy-tale belief that real conditions can change by simply wishing that they change.
45. Morrison, *Tar Baby*, 144.
46. Ibid., 186.
47. Ibid., 185–86.
48. Ibid., 174.
49. Ibid., 143.
50. Ibid., 175.
51. Ibid., 108.
52. Ibid., 136.
53. Ibid., 159.
54. Ibid., 182.
55. Ibid., 157.
56. Ibid., 191.
57. Ibid., 191.
58. Ibid., 217.
59. Ibid., 225.

60. Ibid., 226.
61. Ibid., 114.
62. Ibid., 257.
63. Virginia Hamilton records that "long ago in certain localities of Georgia, the tar baby was considered an actual living, monstrous creature. The monster was composed of tar and haunted isolated places on the plantation. It would insult people to the point at which they would strike out at it and thus become trapped in its sticky substance." Hamilton, *The People Could Fly*, 19. Being the tar baby of the novel, Jadine insults African people in general and Son in particular by her blind acceptance of capitalist values. In striking out to persuade her of the negativisms of these values, Son becomes trapped. He is the rabbit.
64. See James Coleman's "The Quest for Wholeness in Toni Morrison's *Tar Baby*," *Black American Literature Forum* 20, nn. 1, 2 (Spring–Summer 1986): 71 for his comment on the idealism of Son's solution: "Son does not seem able to adapt his folk ways to the modern world." See also Peter B. Erickson's perceptive remark that "Morrison juxtaposes Son's romanticized, dream-like version of Eloe with the more close-up, qualified view we are given when Son brings Jadine home to visit." Erickson, "Images of Nurturance," 22.
65. Morrison, *Tar Baby*, 234–35.
66. Césaire's comment was quoted in Chinweizu's *The West and the Rest of Us*. More than likely, as editor of *The West*, Morrison was aware of this quote.
67. Chinweizu makes this point throughout *The West*. See p. 303 on the arts as an example. This idea of using our African culture as the foundation and then extracting the positive from our traditional, Euro-Christian, and Islamic experiences was best voiced by Dr. Kwame Nkrumah in 1964: "The philosophy that must stand behind this [African] social revolution is that which I have referred to as philosophical consciencism; consciencism is the map in intellectual terms of the disposition of forces which will enable African society to digest the Western and the Islamic and the Euro-Christian elements in Africa, and develop them in such a way that they fit into the African personality. The African personality is itself defined by the cluster of humanist principles which underlie the traditional African society." Nkrumah, *Consciencism*, 79.
68. Discussing the significance of collectivism to the Eloe community, Morrison states: "I don't think two parents can raise a child. You really need the whole village. And if you don't have it, you'd better make it." Wilson, "Conversation," 86. This statement is testament to Morrison's knowledge of and appreciation for the traditional African way of life.
69. Morrison, *Tar Baby*, 264. Various critics have offered their analysis of the ending of *Tar Baby* as well as previous Morrison endings. Most agree that they are unsatisfactory. Perhaps the most insightful of these theories is that of Lounsberry and Hovet and Keith Byerman. Referring to the ending of *Sula*, Lounsberry and Hovet point out that Morrison "carefully refrains from offering a synthesis of her dialectic between the new and the old. She settles for a clear presentation of the limitations of both." Lounsberry and Hovet, "Principles of Perception," 129. Referring to *Tar Baby*, Byerman writes that both Jadine and Son "in effect denies [sic] history: Son by believing in the possibility of returning to a prewhite black purity and Jadine by assuming that blackness was merely an aberration from the truth of Eurocentric Progress." Byerman, *Fingering the Jagged Grain*, 215.
70. Morrison, *Tar Baby*, 90.

71. Ibid., 89.

72. Ibid., 69–70.

73. Morrison reveals another qualitative dimension in the structure of *Tar Baby*. In being a work that has the entire "village" participating in the telling of the story, it becomes a "sort of call-and-response thing that goes on—the narrator functions as chorus." Wilson, "Conversation," 86.

74. In highlighting Son's role as a revolutionary or Christ figure, Morrison arranges his arrival around the Christmas holiday and names the Street house L'Arbe des la Croix (the tree of the cross).

Chapter 6. *Beloved:* Solidarity as Solution

1. Toni Morrison attributes another reason for her ambiguous endings. According to the author, "I could always write thirty more pages or fifty more pages, but I wanted to shift the ending away from the notion of a novel as tell me all I need to know and what is the solution to the problem. . . . I want the reader to think about it, I want him to take some responsibility for the ending." Kay Bonetti, "An Interview with Toni Morrison," (Columbia, Mo: American Audio Prose Library, May 1983). This reason, although perhaps partly accurate, does not address the author's own need to think about the contents of the novel and her own inability to perceive her developing protagonist's next step while writing about his or her present stage. An incubation period is needed. Also, her explanation contradicts her own admission—in the same interview—that when she knows a thing, she feels she should share it with her readers.

2. Self-isolation, not forced isolation, is the culprit. According to Morrison, forced isolation is uncontrollable. Pilate, born without a navel, and Shadrack, made mentally unstable by World War I, represent African people who are unwilling exiles.

3. Thomas LeClair, "The Language Must Not Sweat," *The New Republic* (21 March 1981): 26.

4. Nkrumah, *Consciencism*, 72:

> Capitalism is a development by refinement from feudalism, just as feudalism is a development by refinement from slavery. The essence of reform is to combine a continuity of fundamental principle, with a tactical change in the manner of expression of the fundamental principle. Reform is not a change in the thought, but one in its manner of expression, not a change in what is said but one in idiom. In capitalism, feudalism suffers, or rather enjoys reform, and the fundamental principle of feudalism merely strikes new levels of subtlety. In slavery, it is thought that exploitation, the alienation of the fruits of the labour of others, requires a certain degree of political and forcible subjection. In feudalism, it is thought that a lesser degree of the same kind of subjection is adequate to the same purpose. In capitalism, it is thought that a still lesser degree is adequate. . . . Capitalism is but the gentleman's method of slavery.

5. Toni Morrison, *Beloved* (New York: Alfred A. Knopf, 1987), 136–37.

6. Ibid., 147.

7. Ibid., 3.

8. Ibid., 49.

9. Unlike Milkman, who never struggles for his people, or Son, who gives up with his first failure, Paul D demonstrates the unwavering principles of the revolutionary cadre. Overcoming the dehumanization and emasculation suffered from wearing a horse's bit, from squatting in muddy water that he slept and peed in, and from failing at his first attempt to struggle with Sethe, he comes back to struggle to build a life in the community with Sethe.

10. Morrison, *Beloved*, 39.

11. Ibid., 264.

12. Ibid., 274.

13. Ibid., 185.

14. Ibid., 88.

15. According to the Virginia Hamilton myth of the flying African, the African with the knowledge of flight used his awareness to help other Africans fly. See note 70 in chapter 4.

16. Morrison, *Beloved*, 110.

17. One method Morrison uses to juxtapose today's dilemma with that of slavery is her creation of Sweet Home, a microcosmic analogy to the United States. According to Sethe, she and the Sweet Home men were treated like favored pets instead of beasts of burden. Moreover, in appearance, Sweet Home seemed like heaven instead of hell: "It rolled itself out before her in shameless beauty. It never looked as terrible as it was and it made her wonder if hell was a pretty place too. Fire and brimstone all right, but hidden in lacy gloves" (p. 6). For the African in the United States, Sweet Home is a reminder of life in the United States in the 1980s. Today, Africans live "isolated in a wonderful lie," thinking they are free and successful while having no real control of their destiny and while all around them other Africans are suffering and dying.

18. Ella, enslaved by a European slavemaster and his son, is kept in a locked room for a year. She tells Sethe that what those two did to her that year was unimaginable.

19. Morrison, *Beloved*, 68, 131.

20. Ibid., 17.

21. Ibid., 17.

22. Ibid., 39.

23. There are minor male characters who have positive relationships with women. Wiley Wright in *Sula* and Henry Porter and Macon Dead, Sr. (Sing's husband) in *Song of Solomon* are examples.

24. Morrison, *Beloved*, 273.

25. Ibid., 161.

26. Also, Morrison presents the struggle of another couple as an example for men and women today. Never believing like the others that freedom could exist for some Africans while others are enslaved, walking miles to be with each other, and finding completion only in the other's presence, Sixo and the Seven-Mile Woman sacrifice themselves to create a "free" offspring: Seven-O.

27. Williams, *Capitalism and Slavery*, 7.

28. According to Eric Williams, "The immediate successor of the Indian . . . was not the Negro but the poor white. These white servants included a variety of types. Some were indentured servants, so called because, before departure from the homeland, they had signed a contract, indented by law, binding them to service for a stipulated time in return for their passage." Williams, *Capitalism and Slavery*, 9.

29. Morrison, *Beloved*, 34.

30. Ibid., 34.
31. Ibid., 34.
32. Ibid., 111.
33. Ibid., 112.
34. Rodney, How Europe Underdeveloped Africa, 100.
35. Morrison, Beloved, 139.
36. Ibid., 146.
37. Ibid., 4.
38. Ibid., 180.
39. Morrison, Tar Baby, 186.
40. Morrison, Beloved, 235.
41. Ibid., 95.
42. Ibid., 254, 221.
43. Ibid., 118.
44. It is also interesting to note that Beloved is the first work in which Morrison omits even page numbers. Only the odd pages are numbered. Perhaps such a structural omission is intended to enhance the thematic emphasis on the plight of African people. Certainly, their continual cycle of oppression—including slavery, the slave trade, and colonialism, the underdevelopment of Africa, the distortion of African history, the present destruction of family life, the genocide of men, women, and children—reflects an odd, abnormal existence.
45. Morrison, Beloved, 8.
46. Morrison's structural technique of unveiling pieces of information functions also as a shock absorber. So cruel and vicious was/is the plight of African people that pieces of it must be exposed bit by bit. Sethe and Paul D give each other pieces of their stories at a time so as not to overwhelm the other.
47. Morrison, Beloved, 115.
48. Ibid., 63, 60.
49. Ibid., 216.
50. Ibid., 274–75. At first, the epilogue seems a digression, an unnecessary appendage. However, in light of Morrison's developing canon, it is just as significant to the theme and structure as any other section of the novel. The ending, through repetition, reaffirms to the reader that African people must build on their past, not be haunted by it, that the negative must be dealt with and forgotten, that the positive, i.e., solidarity in the face of extreme oppression, must be remembered and accomplished again. It is a clear reflection of Morrison's advanced consciousness.
51. Morrison, Beloved, 157.
52. Ibid., 205.
53. Ibid., 96.
54. Ibid., 177.

Chapter 7. A Rationalization for and an Assessment of Toni Morrison's Developing Class Consciousness

1. Kay Bonetti, "An Interview with Toni Morrison" (Columbia, Mo.: American Audio Prose Library, 1983). Henceforth, the name "American Audio" will be used to refer to this interview.
2. Morrison, Tar Baby, 181.

3. American Audio.

4. American Audio.

5. Karl Marx, *The Communist Manifesto*, in *Essential Works of Marxism*, ed. Arthur P. Mendel (New York: Bantam Book, 1961), 31.

6. Clenora Hudson, "The Unearthing of Emmett Till: A Compelling Process," *The Iowa Alumni Review* 41, no. 5 (October 1988): 19.

7. Cleveland Sellars, *The River of No Return* (New York: William Morrow & Company, 1973), 60.

8. Ibid., 59.

9. Chinweizu, *The West and the Rest of Us*, 403.

10. Morrison, *Tar Baby*, 174.

11. Chinweizu, *The West and the Rest of Us*, 407.

12. Ibid., 408–9.

13. Ibid., 408.

14. Annie Dillard, "Write Till You Drop," *New York Times Book Review*, 28 May 1989, 23.

15. Eleanor Traylor, "Henry Dumas and the Discourse of Memory," *Black American Literature Forum* 22, no. 2 (Summer 1988): 372.

16. Ellison, Haley, Bambara, Dumas, and Harris are only five writers whose ideas more than likely impacted Morrison. African writers born on the continent had a tremendous impact upon her as well. From them she learned the art of telling a circular, oral story to her people. To her, it seemed that the African novelists in the United States were talking to a European audience rather than an African audience because their novels explained a lot. From African writers on the continent she learned "technique and style; the formation of sentences and the choice of words . . . the kinds of metaphors they chose." American Audio.

17. Alex Haley, *Roots: The Saga of an American Family* (New York: Dell Publishing Co., 1976), 10.

18. Morrison, *Song of Solomon*, 341.

19. Toni Cade Bambara, *The Salt Eaters* (New York: Random House, 1980), 255.

20. Morrison, *Tar Baby*, 222.

21. Ibid., 223.

22. Henry Dumas, *Goodbye, Sweetwater* (New York: Thunder's Mouth Press, 1988), xiv.

23. Toni Morrison, "On Behalf of Henry Dumas," *Black American Literature Forum* 22, no. 2 (Summer 1988): 310.

24. Henry Dumas, "Ark of Bones," in *Goodbye, Sweetwater*, 18.

25. Morrison, *Beloved*, 51.

26. Eleanor Traylor first mentions this connection between the name of Dumas's hometown and Morrison's name for the plantation in *Beloved* in "Henry Dumas." There is also the likelihood that the impact of this name was greatly enhanced by Morrison's awareness of the old classic blues song, "Sweet Home."

27. Morrison, *Beloved*, 6.

28. Already at the back of Morrison's mind was the Plum story in *Sula*. Eva kills her "beloved baby boy" to save him from the living death of heroin just as Sethe kills her baby girl Beloved to save her from the living death of slavery. See p. 34 of *Sula* and p. 163 of *Beloved*.

29. Morrison, *Beloved*, 110.

30. Tate, "Toni Morrison," 130.

31. Bakerman, " 'The Seams Can't Show,' " 56.

32. LeClair, "The Language Must Not Sweat," 25.

33. American Audio.

34. LeClair, "The Language Must Not Sweat," 29.

35. W. E. B. DuBois, quote in Howard Fuller's *Journey to Africa* (Chicago: Third World Press, 1971), 70.

36. Marcus Garvey, "The African Republic and White Politics," in *Voices of a Black Nation: Political Journalism in the Harlem Renaissance*, ed. T. Vincent (San Francisco: Ramparts, 1973), 272–73.

37. Malcolm X, "Malcolm X: Struggle for Freedom," Filmed Interview of Malcolm X in Paris (New York: Grove Press, 1964).

38. Nkrumah, *Class Struggle in Africa*, 87.

39. Stokely Carmichael, *Stokely Speaks* (New York: Random House, 1971), 223.

40. Marcus Garvey, *The Philosophy and Opinions of Marcus Garvey or Africa for the Africans* (London: Frank Cass, 1967), 52.

41. Kwame Nkrumah, *Revolutionary Path* (New York: International Publishers, 1973), 183.

Bibliography

Akpata, Bantole. "Philosphical Consciencism: Its Egalitarian and Humanist Aspects Analysed." *Pan-African Review* 1, no. 2 (1964): 41–42.

Bakerman, Jane. " 'The Seams Can't Show': An Interview with Toni Morrison." *Black American Literature Forum* 12, no. 2 (Summer 1978): 56–66.

Bambara, Toni Cade. *The Salt Eaters.* New York: Random House, 1980.

Barksdale, Richard K. "*Song of Solomon.*" *World Literature Today* 52 (Summer 1978): 465.

Benston, Kimberly W. "I Yam What I Am: the Topos of Un(Naming) in Afro-American Literature." In *Black Literature and Theory,* edited by Henry Louis Gates, Jr. New York: Methuen, 1984.

Bonetti, Kay. "An Interview with Toni Morrison." Columbia, Mo.: American Audio Prose Library, May 1983.

Burns, Emile. *An Introduction to Marxism.* New York: International Publishers, 1966.

Byerman, Keith E. *Fingering the Jagged Grain: Tradition and Form in Recent Black Fiction.* Athens: The University of Georgia Press, 1985.

———. "Intense Behaviors: The Use of the Grotesque in *The Bluest Eye* and *Eva's Man.*" *CLA Journal* 25 (June 1982): 447–57.

Carmichael, Stokely. *Stokely Speaks: Black Power Back to Pan-Africanism.* New York: Random House, 1971.

Chinweizu. *The West and the Rest of Us: White Predators, Black Slaves and the African Elite.* New York: Random House, 1975.

Christian, Barbara. *Black Feminist Criticism.* New York: Pergamon Press, 1985.

———. "Community and Nature: The Novels of Toni Morrison." *The Journal of Ethnic Studies* 7 (1980): 4, 65–78.

Coleman, James. "The Quest for Wholeness in Toni Morrison's *Tar Baby.*" *Black American Literature Forum* 20, nn. 1–2 (Spring–Summer 1986): 62–73.

Davis, Cynthia. "Self, Society, and Myth in Toni Morrison's Fiction." *Contemporary Literature* 23, n. 3 (Summer 1982): 323–42.

De Weever, Jacqueline. "The Inverted World of Toni Morrison's *The Bluest Eye* and *Sula.*" *CLA Journal* 22, n. 4 (June 1979): 402–14.

Dillard, Annie. "Write Till You Drop." *The New York Times Book Review,* 28 May 1989, 23.

DuBois, W. E. B. Quoted in Howard Fuller's *Journey to Africa.* Chicago: Third World Press, 1971.

Dumas, Henry. *Goodbye, Sweetwater.* New York: Thunder's Mouth Press, 1988.

Eliade, Mircea. *Myth and Reality.* Translated by Willard R. Trask. New York: Harper and Row, 1960.

Ellison, Ralph. *Invisible Man*. New York: Vintage Books, 1972.

Erickson, Peter B. "Images of Nurturance in Toni Morrison's *Tar Baby*." *CLA Journal* 28, no. 1 (September 1984): 11–32.

Fanon, Frantz. *The Wretched of the Earth*. New York: Grove Press, 1963.

Fuller, Howard. *Journey to Africa*. Chicago: Third World Press, 1971.

Garvey, Marcus. "The African Republic and White Politics." *Negro World* 12 February 1921. Reprinted in T. Vincent, ed. *Voices of a Black Nation: Political Journalism in the Harlem Renaissance*. San Francisco: Ramparts, 1973.

———. *The Philosophy and Opinions of Marcus Garvey*. London: Frank Cass, 1967.

Haley, Alex. *Roots: The Saga of an American Family*. New York: Dell Publishing Co., 1976.

Hamilton, Virginia. *The People Could Fly: American Black Folktales*. New York: Alfred A Knopf, 1985.

Harris, Barbara. "Myth as Structure in Toni Morrison's *Song of Solomon*." *Melus* 7, n. 3 (Fall 1980): 71.

Harris, Leslie A. "Myth as Structure in Toni Morrison's *Song of Solomon*. *Multi-Ethnic Literature of the U.S.* 7, n. 3 (Fall 1980): 69–76.

Hovet, Grace Ann, and Barbara Lounsberry. "Flying as Symbol and Legend in Toni Morrison's *The Bluest Eye, Sula*, and *Song of Solomon*. *CLA Journal* 27, n. 2 (December 1983): 119–140.

Hudson, Clenora. "Emmett Till: The Impetus for the Modern Civil Rights Movement." Ph.D. diss., University of Iowa, 1988.

———. "The Unearthing of Emmett Till: A Compelling Process." *The Iowa Alumni Review* 41, n. 5 (October 1988): 18–23.

Ikoku, S. G. "Aspects of Consciencism." *Pan-African Review* 1, n. 2 (1964): 94–102.

Klotman, Phyllis R. "Dick-and-Jane and the Shirley Temple Sensibility in *The Bluest Eye*." *Black American Literature Forum* 13, n. 4 (Winter 1979): 123–25.

Lange, Bonnie Shipman. "'Toni Morrison's Rainbow Code." *Critique* 24 (Spring 1983): 173–81.

LeClair, Thomas. "The Language Must Not Sweat." *The New Republic* (21 March 1981): 25–29.

Lee, Dorothy H. "*Song of Solomon*: To Ride the Air." *Black American Literature Forum* 16, n. 2 (Summer 1982): 64–70.

Lester, Julius. *Black Folktales*. New York: Grove Press, 1969.

Lounsberry, Barbara, and Grace Ann Hovet. "Principles of Perception in Toni Morrison's *Sula*. *Black American Literature Forum* 13, n. 4 (Winter 1979): 126–29.

Machel, Samora. "Establishing People's Power to Serve the Masses." In *Samora Machel: An African Revolutionary*, edited by Barry Munslow. London: Zed Books, Ltd., 1985.

"Malcolm X: Struggle for Freedom." Filmed Interview of Malcolm in Paris. New York: Grove Press, 1964.

Marx, Karl. *The Communist Manifesto*. In *Essential Works of Marxism*, edited by Arthur P. Mendel. New York: Bantam Books, 1961.

Bibliography

McClain, Ruth Rambo. "Sula." Black World (June 1974): 51–53, 85.

McDowell, Edwin. "Behind the Best Sellers—Toni Morrison." New York Times Book Review, 5 July 1981, 18.

Middleton, Harris, et al. The Black Book. New York: Random House, 1974.

Morrison, Toni. Beloved. New York: Alfred A. Knopf, 1987.

———. The Bluest Eye. New York: Washington Square Press, 1970.

———. "On Behalf of Henry Dumas." Black American Literature Forum 22, n.2 (Summer 1988): 310–12.

———. Sula. New York: New American Library, 1973.

———. Song of Solomon. New York: New American Library, 1977.

———. Tar Baby. New York: New American Library, 1981.

Ngugi, Thiong'O Wa. Homecoming: Essays on African and Caribbean Literature, Culture and Politics. New York: Lawrence Hill and Company, 1972.

Nichols, Julie J. "Patterns in Toni Morrison's Novels." English Journal 72 (January 1983): 46–48.

Nkrumah, Kwame. Class Struggle in Africa. New York: International Publishers, 1970.

———. Consciencism: Philosphy and Ideology for De-Colonization. New York: Modern Reader, 1964.

———. Revolutionary Path. New York: International Publishers, 1973.

Ogunyemi, Chikwenye O. "Order and Disorder in Toni Morrison's The Bluest Eye." Critique 19, n. 1 (1977): 112–20.

Parker, Bettye J. "Complexity: Toni Morrison's Women—An Interview Essay." In Sturdy Black Bridges, edited by Roseann Bell, Bettye J. Parker, and Beverly Guy-Sheftall. New York: Anchor Press, 1979.

Rodman, Selden. "Whites and Blacks." National Review (26 June 1981): 730–32.

Rodney, Walter. How Europe Underdeveloped Africa. Dar es Salaam: Tanzania Publishing House, 1972.

Sellars, Cleveland. The River of No Return. New York: William Morrow and Company, 1973.

Smith, Barbara. "Beautiful, Needed, Mysterious." Freedomways 14 (First Quarter 1974): 69–72.

Stein, Karen F. "I Didn't Even Know His Name: Names and Naming in Toni Morrison's Sula." Names (September 1980): 226–29.

———. "Toni Morrison's Sula: A Black Woman's Epic." Black American Literature Forum (Winter 1984): 146–50.

Stepto, Robert E. "'Intimate Things in Place': A Conversation with Toni Morrison." In Chant of Saints, edited by Michael S. Harper and Robert E. Stepto. Urbana: University of Illinois Press, 1979.

Tate, Claudia. "Toni Morrison." Black Women Writers at Work, edited by C. Tate. New York: Continuum, 1985.

Toure, Sekou. "Africa on Walk: Revolution and Religion." International Ideological Symposium. Conakry, Guinea, November 13–16, 1978.

Traylor, Eleanor. "Henry Dumas and the Discourse of Memory." Black American Literature Forum 22, n. 2 (Summer 1988): 365–78.

van Gennep, Arnold. *The Rites of Passage.* Chicago: University of Chicago Press, 1960.

Wegs, Joyce M. "Toni Morrison's *Song of Solomon:* A Blues Song." *Essays in Literature* 9, n. 2 (Fall 1982): 211–23.

Williams, Eric. *Capitalism and Slavery.* New York: G. P. Putnam's Sons, 1944.

Williams, Michael W. "Nkrumahism as an Ideological Embodiment of Leftist Thought within the African World." *Journal of Black Studies* 15, n. 1 (September 1984): 117–34.

Willis, Susan. "Eruptions of Funk: Historicizing Toni Morrison." In *Black Literature and Literary Theory,* edited by Henry Louis Gates, Jr. New York: Methuen, 1984.

Wilson, Judith. "A Conversation with Toni Morrison." *Essence* 12 (July 1981): 84, 86, 128, 130, 133, 134.

Index